MW00436298

The Climb of Your Life

Books by Ken Jones

God Happened to Be in the Neighborhood

When You're All Out of Noodles

The Climb of Your Life

Ken Jones

Fleming H. Revell
A Division of Baker Book House
Grand Rapids, Michigan 49516

Published by Fleming H. Revell
a division of Baker Book House Company
P.O. Box 6287, Grand Rapids, MI 49516-6287

Printed in the United States of America

Library of Congress Cataloging-in-Publication Data

Jones, Ken, 1946–
The climb of your life / Ken Jones.
p. cm.
Includes bibliographical references (p.).
ISBN 0-8007-1728-7 (cloth)
1. Meditations. 2. Jones, Ken, 1946– . I. Title.
BV4832.2.J6445 1996
242—dc20 96-20793

To Mom and Dad
with love

Contents

Acknowledgments

There are a number of people I need to thank for making this book a reality. Thank you . . .

To Randee, Marcus, Nathan, and Simeon. The treasure you represent to me as my wife and children cannot be expressed.

To the congregation of Neighborhood Church. "Committed to the Climb" has been our theme for many months now. Thanks for letting me take the time to write some of these thoughts so that others could be encouraged as well.

To the pastors and staff I work with every day: Gary Baker, Gary Miller, Ron Nelson, and Marcus

Jones. Climbing with you as companions is an honor. I trust you with my life.

To every man who is part of my Guard 'n Watch prayer team. Your unselfish prayer and concern for your pastor made this book possible.

To my agents, Tom Thompson and Sealy Yates. Tom walked around a small lake in southern California with me one afternoon and encouraged me to write about The Climb. I love you, buddy.

To Linda Holland, editor, friend, writer . . . and someone who has influenced me to write from the beginning. Thanks, too, to Jim Vincent for your editorial hand.

To my secretary, Connie Miller, who proofread, edited, commented, and answered a bazillion phone calls for me in the process of writing this book. You are, quite simply, excellent.

And finally, I appreciate my mentors and other respected men who have affected my life by their commitment to The Climb: Otis Keener, Noel Wilson, Dick Foth, Silas Gaither, Roger Mahany, Ward Tanneberg, Earl Heverly, all the men in my Tuesday prayer group, and all the pastors in the Greater Modesto Ministerial Association prayer group. Because of all of you, I will never be the same.

Prologue

Once, not so long ago for God I suppose, he did a very strange thing. On an ordinary day, the Lord, the Son of God, prepared to take his leave of heaven. I cannot say what the weather was like the day he left, but it must have been still—still as an infant's yawn.

"What are you doing?" they must have asked him. Those heavenly hosts who tended him day and night had never seen such a strange and witless thing from their all-knowing God. For as they watched, he disrobed. In front of them—shameless as a naked baby—he, the living God of all creation, stood poised and prepared for immortal manhood.

Such a foreign thought: The Supreme Confident was now approachable, naked, and alone.

"Where are you going?" they must have asked him. *Leave? Now? This royal Prince? Dressed like that? The shame of it all. Could he not see the shame of exposing himself to gaping eyes?*

"Let us dress you, Sovereign," they implored. "Won't you take a cloak or robe?"

"No," said the Lord of All. "I'll have no need of a robe. Swaddling clothes will do nicely, thank you."

Swaddling clothes? An old blanket torn into rags? But they did not question. Their only desire: to obey.

I do not know what their curious minds supposed. But I can imagine. And I imagine they asked an honest and innocent question.

"Where, holy Lord? Where are you going?"

And now, he answered in tones of compassion and understanding, language steeped in love.

"I am going for a climb," said the Prince.

The angels puzzled among themselves about this unusual declaration. *A climb? Where? How? How could he who is the First and Last—the Creator of every high and lofty venue—climb any higher?*

The Son noticed their silent wonderings and answered them by raising his arm and pointing. The Prince of Peace stretched and reached and pointed down toward a dark and lonely place.

"There," said the royal Prince.

"There? But Lord," they must have said, "that is a *manger*. Such a small place for Infinite Light to rest. Such a rude and sorry site." A dark place, indeed, soaked with the smell of dung and urine, an acrid stench not fit to pass his royal senses.

And then it happened. He could wait no longer.

At that moment—at that very moment in time—a barefoot Prince, the sovereign Lord of all eternity, stepped into the funk and futility of feeble men. He walked unashamedly across that cold threshold of time and space and willingly climbed into his bed of straw and servanthood.

One of the angels began a chorus. "Joy to the world, the Lord is come. Let heaven and nature sing . . ."

And all the angels joined in unison.

And heaven and nature sang.

And the Light of the world was born.

Hell squinted at the brightness. The light of that Son drove devils from their ghoulish slumber. They sheepishly peeked at this resting, naked Lamb. "Shame on you," said the demons. "Shame! Shame on you!"

And the Lamb of God said, "Yes. Yes, I know."

Introduction

About six weeks ago, my dad called. That wasn't unusual; we talk often. My folks live in southern Illinois and my wife and I live in California with our three sons, so we try to stay in touch by phone as often as possible (though not often enough for my mother). No, it wasn't unusual for my dad, a retired carpenter, to call. He chatted casually about the cold weather they were having. I filled the first several moments of our conversation with news of my trivial pursuits and unimportant matters. But after several moments of mutual exchange, there came a lull in our conversation. A slight, uncomfortably pregnant pause passed between us. And then he said it. He said that awful word.

Such a short word, really. Doctors, of course, know all the large and expansive words that fit this malady. But for those of us who don't own medical dictionaries, physicians combine and distill all those terms into one short, yet pain-filled, six-letter reality: *cancer*. My dad told me his doctors had discovered that he had cancer. They planned surgery in about five weeks, he said. "After that . . ."

And then another pregnant pause.

Another miserable moment. Another second to catch my breath and wait . . . to hear the rest.

That was six weeks ago.

Last week, I waited again. I sat in a hospital cafeteria in Granite City, Illinois . . . waiting for my dad. Actually, I wasn't waiting for my dad. I was waiting for his doctor, waiting for a surgery to end and a recovery to begin. Too impatient to sit in that tiny patient waiting room with the rest of my family, I walked to the cafeteria for a cup of coffee. And as I sat sipping hot black coffee, three floors above me a team of masked men and women I did not even know huddled around my dad. My only dad.

Alone.

He faced this climb without his family standing around watching. We could not come. Doctors didn't need sentimental civilians like us peering over their shoulders, questioning what was going on. They had work to do. A dread disease was being excised. How odd that such a mission of mercy could make one feel so isolated and alone, insulated from the warmth of family by an operating room of cold sterility.

"Are you afraid?" I had asked him just before he left his room.

"Yes, I'm nervous," said my dad, as he reached to take my hand.

An honest admission to his son. My dad's fear had cracked the window of pain in his soul to let an heir in. It was nearly time for the orderlies to come, nearly time for The Climb. I looked down at my dad in that pallid, stark bed, and I prayed. My brothers, my sister, and my mother joined me.

I held his hand as I prayed. I had forgotten how rough a carpenter's hands can be. Rough from weathered work. Gnarled and mashed, time after time. I cradled his hand in mine, and I prayed.

Then a hospital orderly wheeled my dad down the hall. Into the elevator. Climb. Climb. Climb. Have you noticed? Have you ever noticed how slowly hospital elevators move? *What is the holdup? Don't they know? Don't they understand that we need to get this over with so that the family called Jones can get on with life?*

Then a nurse pushed him toward the edge. His destination was an operating suite, where the medical team would take out one of his kidneys—the cancerous one, the one they were worried about. I sat for four hours that day waiting for word about my dad, and the day turned into one of the darkest nights I've ever spent. Finally, a doctor clad in paper booties and green medical garb came and sat down to talk with all of us.

"Good news," he said. "We removed the kidney and surrounding tissue. It looks clear, and I believe he is cancer-free." We breathed. Four hours was a long time to have held our breath, and now, my family breathed again. The doctor continued to drone on about pathology reports and other matters for several more moments, but we had already received the essential truth we listened for. After hearing all that this mere man-physician had to say, my mother spoke. The matriarch expressed her faith.

"Isn't that just like Jesus?" she said, a question that needed no answer in her mind. The doctor looked perplexed at her statement, but we knew what she meant. We, who are family and tied by name and blood, understood her faith.

But that was last week.

Since then, I have been wondering. She does not know it, but her words have been ruminating around in my mind for several days now. What if the results of last week had been different? What if pathology and theology had collided in irreconcilable differences? What if the doctor's announcement had not been good? What then? What of my dear mother's pronouncement? Would a bad report or a tragic end be any less "like Jesus"?

I think not. For his plan is not only to walk alongside us toward our final destinations, but also to help those who are locked in a climb for their lives to persevere and grow and change, regardless of whether the "news" is good or bad. He wants to mature our trust in him, and trust and faith seem to grow best along the slopes of the uphill, daily trek.

Walk with me through these few pages and you will see. This God in flesh—this Carpenter with rough and gnarled hands—beckons those who will commit to follow him. He who climbed down from heaven's splendor to take his place among men begins his ascent. Slow and measured, he climbs. He climbs toward the wilderness hills to be tempted. He climbs the mount to teach those who dare to follow. He marches up a summit to feed the hungry multitudes. He traverses a mountain of opposition and isolation. He prays on the Mount of Olives. Calling. Reaching. Challenging his climbing companions, those who will be tethered to him by name and blood.

Sin's dread disease must be excised. Higher and higher he climbs, until he reaches the summit of Calvary and stretches his arms across the gulf between God and man—heaven's bridge, suspended throughout time.

Listen carefully, and you may hear it . . . a distant, holy noise . . .

The sound of commitment to the climb . . .

The sound of pitons being driven into the Rock of Ages.

And his clear and clarion voice calling, "Follow me."

1
Thresholds

I once read an ancient Danish proverb: "The most difficult mountain to cross is the threshold." If that is what Danish people are taught to believe when they are young, they must be very wise when they are old. I will tell you what I mean.

When I was a little boy, I knew something. Even though the Bible never mentioned it, I was convinced that soon after God created the heavens and the earth, he said, "Let there be school." And there was school. Although I never heard a preacher talk about it, I was convinced that God's response to the fall of man had three distinct and irrevocable consequences:

1. Man would have to earn his living by the sweat of his brow.

2. A woman's sorrow would be greatly increased in childbirth.

3. The children of Adam and Eve and all their descendants—as part of God's judgment—would have to go to school.

Divine retribution started early in my remembrance. From the time I was six years old, it plagued my life from early September until late spring. I remember some of those plagues as if they were yesterday:

- In third grade, listening to Miss Chriss as she explained about some dumb old pottery the Indians used to make.
- My fifth grade affliction, Miss Graham, explaining fractions and how to diagram a sentence (for the umpteenth time).
- Every week—as predictable as a Saturday-night bath—I had a spelling test. And, as if that weren't enough, I felt the sting of a spelling bee once a month. Yuk!

Legalized torture, it was. All done within the confines of one stuffy classroom after another. The curriculum might change from year to year, and the teacher always changed, but the reality never did.

Dull days, looking at my world from the inside out. Daze upon daze, as I stared out the windows of Marshall School, an ancient and awful place. It was in the middle of Granite City, Illinois, a steel town just across the Mississippi River from St. Louis.

Patrolled by all-seeing and nearly omnipotent teachers, Marshall School seemed dark and foreboding, like some medieval castle with dungeons of learning and dragons of boredom.

Marshall School was old when I went there. It has always been old, I think. When I walked the halls of Marshall School, my nose alerted me to the smell of varnished oak floors, musty and aged, seasoned by seasons of learning. Two stories of brown brick with a roof as flat as Illinois bottomland. All summer long, Marshall School sat quiet and empty as a garden tomb.

But then, September. The sound of children and the smell of new clothes.

Each fall, I participated in a familiar ritual for school-aged children everywhere by cutting leaves out of colored construction paper and taping them to our classroom windows. Later, as winter set in, it was one-of-a-kind snowflakes and cotton-ball snowmen; toward spring, we did silhouettes of Abraham Lincoln and kites with colored tails. All this festooning was initiated by well-intentioned teachers who told their wards that such decorations would brighten the building and let passersby know there was life going on inside the place. But they couldn't fool me. I knew better.

This wasn't life. This was death.

This was part of the fall of man.

This was school.

The spring I turned twelve, I spent an eternity in Mr. Meyers's sixth-grade class. Mr. Meyers was tall, and to me his face seemed to have footprints in it. His faced looked for all the world like a road map of where he'd been all his life. The narrow and etched face framed hollow, sunken eyes, potholes of pensive thought. My parents called him "Smiley," although I never could figure out why. He didn't smile much. In fact, most of the time, as I remember, he had a scowl on his face.

I sat next to the windows, right in front of Gary Gann. I was bored stiff. (I don't know about Gary, but I suspect he was too.) In the spring, after a long Midwest winter, when the trees began to bud, the air was warm, and the breeze was blowing, I wondered what on earth I was doing in a stuffy classroom listening to Mr. Meyers talk about geography. I loathed being fastened to my seat like some mere child. I was bored. And besides that, I was twelve years old, nearly grown.

Puberty is a nasty word. I don't mean an obscene word—not a foul, locker-room word, of course. But it's a nasty word. Puberty hits below the belt about twelve or thirteen, knocking the wind out of us. It seems strange to me now. I never remember Mr. Meyers mentioning puberty. He talked about nature and life cycles; he mentioned birds and bees and pollination of flowers. I still don't know much about those things. But I do know that the spring I turned twelve, my thoughts turned to more than the trees that were beginning to bud.

I noticed her.

I enjoyed sitting in front of Gary Gann because we could whisper to each other when Mr. Meyers's back was turned. But I really enjoyed sitting behind Jeanine. Over the course of the summer and fall, she had taken a new shape, a form unexpected and pleasant to my uninitiated eye. How could I have overlooked this obviously delightful person for so long? Hadn't she been in class with me last year? Hadn't she lived in my neighborhood for a long time? Strange. Wasn't she the same Jeanine who kicked my shin in the fourth grade and told me she hated all boys? She seemed civil enough now. Civil and interesting to talk to—and interested. Interested in me. Me, the person. Me, the one sitting behind her. Me . . . the boy standing on the threshold of manhood.

Mr. Mulock, our P.E. teacher, came into our class one day to announce that our school would be part of a multi-school, all-city track and field meet. He discussed the need to train, to work out. After school he would teach us about track and field, he said. I got excited, and for the next several weeks I trained hard.

You see, I had an idea. Jeanine, who was a very fast runner, would also be doing some things in the meet. I thought it would be great if she won the trophy for the girls, and I could win it for the guys. Kind of a "king and queen" thing, you know.

I told my entire family about the race. Every night as I went to bed I thought about it. I dreamed about it. When I walked to school every morning, I broke into a sprint for the last block or so, just to get in some extra training. This was serious stuff, and I knew it. Mr. Mulock had already told us that to win you had to be committed. You had to want to win more than anything else. And I definitely wanted to win. The closer the meet got, the harder I trained.

On the day of the meet, my dad took off from work so he could come watch me run. I was really glad he was there, but I tried not to act too glad. None of the other guys acted glad that their dads and moms were there watching, and I didn't want to seem like some little kid. Mr. Mulock called us all together and read the starting times for all the events.

"You are responsible to be at your appointed events on time," he said. "No one will be baby-sitting you. If you miss your starting time, too bad."

No problem for me. I didn't need a baby-sitter. I was ready. I was committed.

The one-hundred-yard dash would be run at 3:15, and by 3:00, I was already standing around waiting. Finally, a large man with a whistle around his neck and a clipboard in his hand began to speak in a loud voice. A somewhat portly man, he wore a T-shirt that was one size too small and carried a starter's gun in his hip pocket. His very presence commanded respect. He read all the names of the contestants, and I eyed each one as their names were called. I could tell—just by looking, I could tell that I was more committed than them all. As our names were read, we each took our appointed place in the lanes specified. And then it was time.

"Come to your mark."

I knew how to line up. Coach Mulock had shown me how to shake the cinders off my feet and then step into the starting blocks. I placed my hands just behind the chalk line, being careful not to go over that line even one-quarter of an inch. I knew that my family name was on that line. I felt the cinders on my hands. I looked at the other runners. Were their hearts racing, too?

I could see the finish line a hundred yards down the track. Not so far, really. Just a quick dash. *When the gun goes off, I will close my eyes and run,* I thought.

"Set . . ."

And now, the starter raised his gun. Time to prove myself. Time to prove I'm better than the next guy. Time to whisper one final thought to myself and one desperate prayer to God: *Please, dear God. Let me win.* Every muscle poised, taut and tight as a bow string. Heart racing. People watching. My dad watching.

Crack! went the gun.

I ran. With the wind at my back, with the wind filling my sails, I closed my eyes and I ran. In blind, blinding speed, I raced toward the tape and a threshold—my very first attempt at winning a race against the rest of the world.

When I knew I was nearing the finish line, I opened my eyes to lean toward the tape.

Shocked. Disappointed. And besides that, mortified. Dead last. All I could see when I opened my eyes was dust and the flying heels of every other runner. I was in the wrong lane. Running with my eyes closed had caused me to leave my lane, crossing several others as well. By the time I realized my position on the one-hundred-yard course, the race was over.

No king and queen. No ribbon for this victor, just the embarrassment of walking off to the side of a one-hundred-yard dash I hadn't even finished.

"Where were you going?" asked my well-intentioned dad, as he put his arm across my shoulder. "The gun fired and you took off toward that old, red barn across the field. I couldn't tell where you were headed. Weren't you lookin' where you were runnin'?"

"No," I said, my voice trailing off in the wind. He tried to console me. He mentioned that it wasn't the end of the world not to win. He didn't fully understand.

I didn't say it to him at the time, but I wanted to die. Knowing I had not won was difficult, but realizing I hadn't even finished was mortifying. I couldn't even make it one hundred yards. The young warrior in me wanted to evaporate. Disintegrate. Better to die than embarrass my dad. Better to drop dead than have to face Jeanine.

I did not expire that day. I thought I would, but I did not. Instead, I learned. Just as surely as if I had been sitting in some stuffy classroom, I learned. I stepped across a threshold as I failed to cross that line, a difficult mountain indeed. For sometimes, the most challenging climbs do not involve ascending toward a summit of triumph, but crossing a threshold of maturity.

Spring in the City of David. Passover time again. Like all obedient Jewish sons, Jesus went to Jerusalem with his parents for the feast. Twelve years old, a mere child, he would celebrate Passover with his parents and then return home.

Their walk from Nazareth to Jerusalem was not easy. As they walked from Nazareth south toward the feast, they left the pleasant plains of Jezreel and passed into the Judean wilderness. Travelers had to walk mile after mile across sun-baked, barren earth while enduring the searing heat. Dusty and winding, the journey of almost sixty-five miles spanned several days, and the celebrants arrived tired from the trek. But every year, Joseph and Mary and their young son joined thousands of others who walked resolutely toward the gates of the City of David like a serpentine parade; family and friends were on their way to the feast, a journey into the old and ancient ways.

The days of this particular Passover were uneventful, like so many other feasts they had attended. And when the celebration was over, Joseph's clan began the long walk back to Nazareth.

Well, not all of them.

One of them—the twelve year old—stayed behind . . . to go to school. Odd, isn't it, that Omniscience would desire classroom instruction?

But the fall of man made it so.

The temple sat squarely in the middle of Jewish life—ancient halls filled with musty smells of parchment scrolls, walls reverberating the sounds of arguing men. These teachers debated the law like ecclesiastical candidates running for office. Craggy-faced, their countenances were etched with lines. Faces drawn by the gravity of the times. Old men dressed in old robes teaching old ways.

My guess is that these aged ones rarely smiled. There was little for them to rejoice about. Day in and day out, the drone of their voices filled the air as they discussed and questioned and waited. Yes, they waited for him—Messiah, who would come and deliver them from all of their ills.

On an ordinary day one spring, Divine Truth walked among them, pulled up a chair, and sat down to inquire. His nonbearded innocence must have seemed strange and out of place among them as he sat listening and learning and asking questions that amazed them. Perhaps their cloudy daze brightened, as God's Light fell in the midst of these mere and unsuspecting men. His very words permeated the petrified magnificence of the temple courts.

All of the people marveled at how wise he was and his knowledge and handling of the Scriptures.

But the boy wonder didn't enjoy his platform for long. His parents showed up looking for him. And they didn't treat him like God in the flesh. They scolded him, like he was some naughty boy who had stayed out too late. I wonder what it must have been like for Jesus to have all the leaders and teachers hear his mother ask him, "Why have you treated us like this?" Was he embarrassed? How did it feel to have his mom and dad walk into the Father's house and tell him it was time to go home? Was it hard for him to be "dressed down" by his mother in front of these respected men?

Perhaps, but he endured it anyway. Imagine it. God being treated like a child while he was trying to stand up and act like a man.

"Twelve" is an awful thing to happen to a person, especially one so young. And yet, Jesus crossed that threshold of manhood and approached the doorway to servanthood with such dignity and maturity. Even though I cannot comprehend it—my understanding and my faith struggle to imagine it—God sat among men. Supreme and omnipotent . . . and twelve. I will ever be grateful.

There have been many thresholds in my life, many opportunities for development and maturity and growth. Some of them involved my inner man, some of them were more intellectual or physical in nature. I passed through biological puberty once, but my spiritual growth and development has occurred many times over the course of my life. Growing, painful times. How about you? Ever had a confusing time? A season when you didn't understand the changes happening deep within you, divinely ordered times when you were stretched, tested, and matured? Of course you have. It's a recurring part of The Climb that we cannot avoid.

During those times and in those seasons we can be most grateful that there was a day when God—God incarnate and infinite—was twelve years old. God the boy walked across the mountain threshold to manhood, and the Father recorded the climb so we could all remember it.

I'm glad Jesus was twelve. I know he was God in the flesh. I know he came as a baby, but I can't really identify with that because I can't remember when I was a baby. But I remember when I was twelve. I remember puberty, pimples, the races I lost, and the manhood I was trying to discover. I know about those things as surely as I know what coffee tastes like.

I could never know how it felt to be Jesus, the only Son of God, but I know how it feels to be twelve. I know how it feels to have your voice change in mid sentence, to be embarrassed at the physical changes that are happening. I know how it feels to suddenly be aware of girls. And I know how it feels to run life's rat race as fast and as hard as I can, and then . . . come away looking like a failure and feeling for all the world like I'm going to die. If you've had a bout with biological or spiritual puberty, maybe you know what I mean.

That's why I'm glad there was a mountain called "twelve." As Jesus sat there in those ancient courts asking questions, he was poised at the threshold, taking his place as a man among men. He modeled obedience and commitment to the Father's plan. And, as one ready to become a man, he demonstrated a firm understanding of the answers to three of life's most challenging questions: "Who am I? Why am I here?" and "Where am I going?"

He knew who he was: He was the only Son of his father. He also knew a day would come when he would take his mark to begin the race. His dad would be watching. His family name would be on the line.

He knew why he was here: He had to be about the Father's business. His mind and his thoughts were on her, his bride-to-be, the church. There would be only one chance for victory and only one race to run.

He knew where he was going: He was preparing for The Climb of his life. Even at twelve years old, he was already aware that to finish The Climb with his eyes wide open, he would have to endure hardship and prejudice along the way. He knew that he would have to cut across the pretentious lines of religious structures and social strata. And at twelve years old, he already knew that if he did not finish his race, it was, indeed, the end of the world.

Perhaps most amazing of all, in the midst of the temple that day as old ones marveled at his questions, this twelve-year-old son of Joseph and Mary—this twelve-year-old Son of God—did more than just *feel* like he was going to die. . . .

He was absolutely convinced of it.

2
The Road Sign

Last night we had a slide show. Nathan, my middle son, went to the hall closet at my request and got some of our most treasured possessions—our slides. We have boxes of slides in our hall closet, boxes marked with cryptic writing on the outside—words like "Vacation 1989" and "General Family, Summer of 1991." If you come to visit us, we won't force our slides on you. We never do that with company. But occasionally we enjoy sitting together and remembering, remembering where we've been and how our three boys have grown.

So last night, we popped some popcorn, arranged our chairs into a mini-amphitheater, and had ourselves a Jones family slide show for nearly two hours.

But last night's showing wasn't only because we had an urge to see some slides. Yesterday afternoon as I sat in my study, a vivid memory came back to me. In fact, the event I remembered had impressed me so much when it occurred that I had taken a slide of it just to make sure I'd never forget the significance of the moment. And last night refreshed my memory as we watched the pictures in the slide box marked "Sabbatical."

Several years ago, my wife and I were privileged to enjoy a sabbatical together. The wonderful congregation we served gave us two months away from our normal responsibilities in order to reflect and recover, to restore our batteries drained from the rigors of pastoral ministry. After much thinking and deliberation, we decided to spend the first three weeks of our sabbatical in the Canadian Rockies. Just the two of us. It was a wonderful gift.

Both of us love mountains, and neither Randee nor I had been to Canada before. We found it to be an unusually beautiful place. Beauty, of course, is a relative thing. I've heard some music that other people had described as beautiful that I didn't think was so great. I've looked at my share of portrait paintings that had eyes in the wrong places and ears that were way too big. Those paintings may have been masterpieces, but they weren't beautiful. But I can tell you as a fact that the Canadian Rockies radiate beauty in a raw and rugged form.

For nearly three weeks of our sabbatical, we enjoyed the wonder of God's creation. We ate out. We slept in. We read C. S. Lewis, Walt Wangerin, and Annie Dillard—insightful authors, gifted writers. We walked along quiet paths and listened to still waters. We held hands. We talked. We smelled wild roses and mountain dogwood in bloom. In essence, we stopped. No phones. No kids. No duties or bills or noise. Nearly three weeks of "nowhere to go, and all day to get there," alone in the Canadian Rockies, surrounded by magnificent beauty.

But what of the slide?

Well, one of our favorite activities during our sabbatical was taking long drives to photograph wildlife. Elk, deer, moose, mountain sheep. We got pictures of all of them. Porcupine, chipmunks, even grizzly bears were fair game for our lenses. But none of our spectacular wildlife photos made me ponder as much as one odd sight.

As we drove one day looking for wild game to photograph, I noticed a sign. A road sign—yellow with a black border that made it hard to miss. Three words I had never seen printed together before were centered on the sign. Three words that surprised me. I stopped the car when I saw the words.

This moment begged further thought and reflection, so I stopped the car, opened my door, leaned across the hood, and snapped the shutter of our camera as I aimed it at the sign . . . a sign that read: "Important Intersection Ahead."

Such a curious and strange message for a sign. I wondered to myself if the reason I had never seen such a sign before was because I had never seen such an intersection before. The words *important* and *intersection* don't seem to fit together to me; they don't seem to belong on the same sign. I've seen "Dangerous Intersection" signs. I've read "Congested Intersection" signs. Once, in Europe, I even saw a sign that had nothing but an exclamation point on it. But never in all my travels had I ever seen a sign that read, "Important Intersection Ahead."

As I got back in the car, I told my wife to keep her eyes open. Something big must be on the horizon.

About a quarter of a mile ahead, there was, indeed, an intersection. Quiet. Almost no traffic. No marker to distinguish it from any other place. Not even a traffic signal. Just a four-way, generic, run-of-the-mill stop sign. We looked squarely in the face of an "Important Intersection" . . . but we had no idea why it was so, why it was so important they had to put up a sign so everyone would know.

I had expected perhaps a plaque. You know, "On this date in the Spring of '47. . ." Or a cemetery where someone famous might be buried, or perhaps the boyhood home of a Canadian patriot. But here at this so-called important intersection, I found not a beautiful scene nor the markings of an ancient site. No, just a four-way, generic, run-of-the-mill stop sign that might just as well have read: "No need to stop—a brief pause will do, since there's nothing to see around here anyway!"

Last night during our time of slides and remembering about our sabbatical, I thought about it again. I never did figure out what was so important about that intersection.

Every day he showed up at one particular bend in the river. He had a habit of wearing camel hair cinched at the waist with a leather belt. John the Baptizer, they called him, a Nazarite who never cut his hair and had peculiar culinary habits—wild field honey and locust. Quite a preacher, too. He baptized people in the Jordan River, preaching repentance for sin.

"Time's up!" he would thunder, as he leveled his cannon-like voice on unsuspecting gawkers. "Change your life. God's kingdom is here." No messing around with this message-wielding courier. Impassioned and impervious to criticism, John chose words that would grab at the throats of hypocritical Pharisees and Sadducees. "Brood of snakes," he called them. Though he said the words in their presence and knew they would want his head for it, John stood his ground, his feet planted firmly in the silt of a river bottom.

If you had been there—standing on the riverbank watching as the parade of people made their way into the water—you might have been tempted to snap a picture of the Baptist. He was quite a character, a real live wild man in action who feared no one. But you'd have been focusing on the stagehand and missing the star—that Humble Man standing in line, waiting his turn.

There was certainly nothing special about him, this Jesus of Nazareth. Some called him an illegitimate carpenter's son, questioning his parentage. He wasn't dressed up, and nothing about his form or visage was notable in any way. My guess is that everyone there walked right on by. They got so caught up in watching a wild-looking baptizer that they missed the Meek One.

It wasn't John's fault, of course. He did everything he could to point folks in the right direction. He consistently tried to tell them that the one to come was "mightier than I" and "I am not fit to untie the thong of his sandals."

Yet the crowd listening to the booming voice of the baptizer almost missed the quiet sound of the Meek One stepping into the water. That must be why God spoke up. It was almost as if God couldn't bear the idea that those watching Jesus being baptized would miss the point, that a commitment so profound as his might go unnoticed, that his climb into the river would go unrecognized by everyone but the baptizer himself. So there, in the middle of the flat plains of Judea, devoid of magnificent scenery, God posted a sign. A one-of-a-kind expression about a once-and-for-all event. A simple sign, really, when you consider the incredible implications of the moment. A sign, written with the quill of a dove's wing and read by God himself: "This is my beloved Son, in whom I am well pleased."

It was almost as if God were saying, "Keep your eyes open. He may not look like much to your sin-dimmed eyes, but don't let that fool you. Don't let your search for rest from The Climb cause you to miss the Unpretentious One who stands waiting his turn. The Prince of heaven now occupies the place of the humble servant, so do not let the eternal significance of this moment escape you." *Unpretentious* is not the same as *unimportant*. God and man have now come together—a "Most Important Intersection Ahead."

Some days, as I follow God in The Climb, I need that reminder. Many times, he posts his purposes and direction for my life in obvious ways. I've seen "Danger" signs. "Out-of-bounds," screams his Word. "Get back in line." And some days, I see "Congested Traffic Ahead" signs. "Slow down; wait your turn," his Word seems to caution. I'm glad for those obvious admonitions.

But there are other days—in fact, most days—when life seems like just another convergence of time and space and "stuff." I know that more significant things are happening, of course. I just don't know what they are. That is often the case with The Climb. No remarkable vistas. No distinguishing landmarks. Not even a traffic signal to hint that it's okay to proceed. Just life, filled with long, sometimes boring lines, lines and litanies of words and thoughts and deeds.

That's why I need to remember the sign "Most Important Intersection Ahead." Significant things are not always marked, but they are always there, whether I recognize them as such or not. Think back on your own life. Isn't it true that some of the most incredible things that have ever come your way appeared when you did not expect them? Some of life's most wonderful happenings and most challenging tests occur in the middle of unmarked and unremarkable intersections of life.

That's one of the great aspects of climbing with him. Jesus has not only been this way before, he now walks alongside us in The Climb. Just as surely as there is a God in heaven, there is a God come to earth who knows and understands it all. He knows my commitment to climb with him, to believe on him, to follow him, and his still and insistent voice brings a firm but encouraging demand every day: "Keep moving. Follow me."

Of course, there are days when I am tempted to question and wonder. I catch myself having a slide show, sitting down to review past scenes, focusing on some of the bad stuff that has happened. I notice the drabness of my life, the unexciting and boring elements of it. And I begin to think it will never change.

Invariably on those days, if I invite him, Jesus will interrupt my pity with a gentle reminder. He walks into my memories and patiently reminds me that there are no ordinary days when I follow an extraordinary God. He points to every single moment and convinces me he is there, even when I can't see him in the picture.

And if I invite him to come and join me in my boring, uneventful life, he brings his assurance that every intersection I enter today will be important to him—even the ones that don't seem to have any significance at all.

3

The Green-Eyed Monster

I saw something recently that sickened me. I saw it with my own eyes, over near the "Christian living" section of our local Christian bookstore. An awful thing, really. The people in the store seemed oblivious to it. Thank God they didn't see it. They walked right on by this dark and shameful thing. But I noticed. And I will tell you what I saw.

I like to think that people who own and operate Christian bookstores have the gift of encouragement. They encourage their fellow Christians by providing an incredible resource of inspiration, information, and tools for The Climb. In our town, we have a great Christian bookstore; in fact, for the past several years, editors of *Christian Retailing* magazine have chosen Beardsley's as one of America's best Christian bookstores. Les Beardsley, the owner, has been a friend of mine for a long time.

The music coming over the sound system is Christian music, and Les prides himself in stocking the latest in Christian music and videos. The entire store radiates a bright and cheery atmosphere, and the clerks take extraordinary pains to make sure that customers feel served and important. I could spend hours just walking up and down the aisles.

A few weeks ago, I needed a particular book for a study I was doing, and I dropped by the bookstore to see if they had what I needed. I walked briskly from my car, mindful of my schedule. Ministry demands had already taken me outside my home three nights in a row, and I had just completed a forty-hour "office" week. Now, after a quick drive home and a quicker shower, my family and I would be off to another ministry venue—a wedding. I couldn't be late. I rushed along, walking up and down the aisles, my tired eyes scanning the titles.

A dozen or so people shared the aisles with me. While I looked for the book I needed, each of the people around me seemed lost in his or her own search for just the right volume, just the right book to meet a particular need. I began to notice them, these fellow searchers. Even though my schedule demanded a certain sense of urgency, I slowed my search, and instead began to watch how the people around me looked for books.

Some of them used their fingers to touch the books before they picked them up. Some of them moved their lips when they read silently. Some stooped to read. They knelt down in their search for a great book. I watched them hold the books—books on how to live a Christian life, how to be devoted to Christ.

And then, as I made my way to the end of one long aisle and into a spacious display area, I saw something else, an awful thing that sickened me. Perhaps I was too tired. Perhaps I wasn't paying attention.

Several people had gathered on the end of the row, surrounding an array of best-selling books. Columns of these books stood like pillars in the middle of the floor, forming a literary colonnade through which people could walk. Other stacks leaned against the wall. Numbers above the stacks indicated which book was the number-one best-seller, which book was number two, which was number three. And all around, people gathered and milled and perused this display of "special" books. They picked up books by Max, Frank, and Chuck. They thumbed through books by James, Pat, and Robert. These were wonderful books; many of them I had already read. Wonderful writers. Great publishers.

No, it was not the mere sight of people looking at best-selling books that sickened me. I love books, especially my own. That was the problem.

For there in the midst of that mingling of words and books and men, a pool of shameful envy welled within my inner man. Invisible and silent as a rising tide, it formed deep within me. I wished for one of my books to be there—there in the midst of the people, there in the middle of admiration and notice. I craved one of those numbers for my own. And as if that weren't black enough, I wished some of those writers didn't have books that were so popular.

Cowardice and shame, of course, would not allow me to say what I was really thinking. But inside my disgusting self, I berated and bludgeoned the work and the names of honorable and gifted men. I uttered a noiseless barrage of words to those who could not hear. *They don't write that well,* I thought. *My books. You need to read what I have written. You, who kneel in the middle of these stacks. You, who lean against these walls for respite from The Climb. You need to hear what* my *pen has to say.*

Thank God they could not hear.

Thank God they could not see this pity-filled man.

And then I left the store. I drove to my home, never finding the book I needed. And then . . . I was ashamed.

William Shakespeare wrote in *Othello* that "Men should be what they seem . . ." (act 3, scene 3). I've always thought he was right, but I became uncomfortably aware of a troubling fact: Deep inside of me I was different from what I seemed. That green-eyed monster of envy that Shakespeare mentioned in *Othello*'s third act had taken up residence in my foolish and careless life.

I told my wife how sorrowed and disappointed I was in myself to think that such things could come from the recesses of my heart. She put her arms around me, kissed my neck, and held me for a long while before she said she understood.

But I'm not sure she understood.

A few days later, I talked to a trusted editor friend of mine about the awful thing I had seen in the bookstore. He told me not to worry. He told me that books are like babies, and that as a proud parent it's okay to want the very best for them. He said it's natural for authors to want their books to do well. Writers pour their lives into creating a book, and then they want others to be helped and encouraged. "It's only natural," he said.

And he said he understood.

But I'm not sure he did.

For the failure that I felt did not flow from a desire to see my books do well. The whole idea behind writing a book is that others will find it, read it, and be encouraged. No, my failure had its roots in a climb. A climb for success. An ascent toward notoriety. My own personal ladder of significance now leaned against the wall of pride and envy.

Finally, I went to him—the sovereign Lord of All. Alone and in the quiet of my time with him, I shared those secret thoughts; I whispered my private failures to One who already knows them all. I told him of my jealousy and of my shame at allowing such unseemly things to be entertained within the walls of my heart—arrogance, a lust for success, and pride. I told him of my sorrow and deep regret at such vain-filled thoughts. He said to me, "I forgive you."

And I believed him.

For as I confessed my failures and repented of my attitudes, he convinced me he already knew how I felt. There was a day when the same green-eyed monster approached Jesus; lust and pride paid him a visit. There was a day when hell's spotlight glared, and the demons dared him to prove he was more than just an aspiring actor pretending to be divine.

And The Climb took him to center stage.

Forty days is a long time to wander around in the desert, driven by the Spirit's wind. Jesus had no warm surroundings. No music from the heavenly hosts. No books to read. No encouragement or help along the way. For forty days, the waving horizons distorted by the desert heat beckoned him to continue his trek. For forty nights, he listened to the wind and felt the chill of the darkness.

He walked across islands of isolation—arid isles, dry and parched. Weakened by hunger's pangs, weathered and wearied. Starved. Starved for sustenance and attention, the solitary figure began the climb up the steep steps of temptation's peak alone.

And yet . . . not alone.

For *he* was there. The tempter came along, sly and cunning. He knew better than to approach this Lion of the tribe of Judah with roaring threats and intimidations. Instead, this trickster, this devil, this lord of darkness changed his tactics for a season. The enemy of our souls prepared a script—words. He would bring reasonable and well-written words, words to soothe the pallet of the half-starved Meek One. He would lay a trap, a well-developed plot. He wrote a short play-on-words of three acts, hoping to see a divine comedy, desperate to see a divine tragedy.

The house must have been full as the curtain rose. For certain, the ghouls of hell came early to get a good seat. They had been waiting a long time for this show to begin. A dark and shadowy figure moved across the stage and opened the action with subtle dialogue.

"Satisfy your hungers," the script began. A weak smile seeped from the lips of the villainous devil. "Someone with your pedigree deserves it. Go ahead. Give a command performance. Tell these rocks you need bread."

The demons of hell leaned forward in their seats. They didn't want to miss the next line of dialogue; they listened hard to what he had to say. And this is what they heard. With clear and truly inspired tones, the Bread of Life said, "There's more to life than bread."

The audience of imps and demons offered no applause for the Bright and Morning Star's profound and truthful statement. Instead, a disappointing murmur rolled through the halls of hell.

Time now for the second act and a scene change—a rooftop in the center of the holy city. The high point of a temple built by the hands of men for God himself. The devil spoke again. "This scene calls for you to jump from the top of the roof, since you are starved for attention. It's okay. The angels are watching. They won't let you stub your precious toe," said the crafty playwright, as he quoted the Scriptures. "See? You wrote it down in your own Book. It says right here . . ." And he pointed at the Book, and dangled a tempting morsel of verse. He knew. All writers love the sight of their own words, and he suspected this Writer was no different.

Applause broke out in the regions of hell. They loved this verbal exchange of word for Word. "Bravo! Brilliant!" they cheered. "Absolutely brilliant." Their champion had staged a trapdoor, and the opponent stood at the edge. But the divine wordsmith would not stumble over a test of such obvious and mortal insecurity. His eternal Word would stand on its own. He had no need to prove his significance. Instead, he answered with his own "It is also written . . ."

And the second test was passed . . . and the second act was done.

Desperate now, the hordes of hell screamed encouragements to their sinister leader. The twists and turns of the action were not following the plot line of the script he had planned. The crafty one grew bold by their encouragement, and he fashioned a final and magnificent change of scene.

"Climb with me," said the wicked one. And they climbed higher and higher. He showed the Committed One of heaven such kings and kingdoms as could not be believed, palaces of splendor and incredible beauty. The success of the world and the sounds of the accolades of men spread before him and reached to the farthest horizons. "Oohs" and "aahs" rose from the galleries and balconies of hell, as envy and desire entered the picture.

But Satan was not finished yet.

He waited. In dramatic style, the prince of darkness waited . . . until no other sound could be heard but his own tempting and reasonable voice. An eerie stillness settled over the foul crowd as they watched. Silence on the stage. Quiet on the set, as he turned to the First and the Last.

"Say the word, and it's all yours," said the evil one.

And so he did. God in flesh spoke his own glorious Word. He knew there would be days when desperate men would kneel in search of a living truth, a Word they could believe and touch, a Word that would touch them. And so, he stepped across the best cellars hell could create. The author of the holy Book, the author and finisher of our faith, he walked to the apron of this world's stage and delivered a line he had written himself, his own purpose-filled soliloquy: "Worship the Lord your God, and serve him only."

And so the curtain fell, as that critic the devil left him for another season. Disappointed demons filed out of the hall . . . while angels gave a standing ovation from the wings.

4

Radical Lessons

You may think it would be easy for a child to distinguish his name from any other, but in my case, things were a bit more complex. (They usually were.) The name "Little Kenny" rang in my ears a lot when I was young. My dad's name is Ken, too, so I guess the "little" added to my name helped my friends and family communicate which Kenny they were talking about. But the day my mother enrolled me in first grade, I heard the name Kenny again—this time, in a totally different context.

I still remember that day and how we walked up the steps to Marshall School. A lady with a clipboard greeted us. She asked for my name and said she would tell us which first-grade class I would be joining. I watched her move her pencil down the list until she found my name. Then she smiled and pointed down the hall to the first room on the left. And as she pointed, she uttered the word Kenny. But she wasn't really saying *my* name. And she wasn't saying my dad's name either. As she pointed to the room, she pronounced my teacher's name. Can you believe it? My very first teacher was Miss Kenny.

Miss Kenny held the position of supreme "ruler" in the first grade. (Which meant that if you didn't behave yourself in her class, she'd give your bottom a supreme whack with a ruler!) I remember thinking that Miss Kenny was old when she taught me. She seemed very old, older than even my mother, who was twenty-seven. But Miss Kenny was a masterful teacher. She taught us letters and numbers. She told us some great stories.

She demonstrated science projects, too. She asked us to bring a sweet potato from home. We stuck toothpicks around the edges of those sweet potatoes and set them in jars of water. Then we carefully lined them up on the windowsill over by the heat radiator and waited to see what would happen. Every day we checked for progress. Within a few weeks, the combination of sunlight and water caused those sweet potatoes to sprout roots. Eventually they matured into green plants. Amazing what I learned in first grade with Miss Kenny.

One of the first things we learned was how to "sit tall." I sat in front of Debbie Spengler, who stood head and shoulders above me when we lined up next to each other at the drinking fountain. But when we sat down at our desks, I was the taller one. Consequently, I loved it when Miss Kenny would say, "Boys and girls, sit tall." When Miss Kenny gave that command, we all knew we needed to snap to attention, place our torsos in alignment with the backs of our chairs, and fold our hands on top of our desks to await further orders. She taught a lot of other things, too, like how to not push in line, how to play nicely on the playground, how to hang your coat on the coatrack. Miss Kenny possessed an uncanny knack for teaching in ways I will never forget.

She also modeled wonderful manners for us. She taught us how to act mature and grown-up. For instance, she told us not to play in the water in the boys' lavatory. But Freddy Roberts was a slow learner. Just after recess one day, when I came into the rest room, he thought it would be funny to squirt me with water. As I walked in, he stuck his first-grade-sized finger into the spout and turned the faucet on, sending a stream of water in my direction. (I definitely remember. He squirted me first.)

Drenched, I ran to a basin for retaliation. Since I was equipped with several first-grade-sized fingers of my own, I shoved one into the spout and commenced firing water at my adversary, Freddy.

However, my aim proved less than accurate. Another classmate, Ronnie Selph, stood watching nearby, and as I directed a spray of water at Freddy, I accidentally squirted Ronnie in the ear. He squealed and ran to a basin of his own to join the skirmish. The battle raged for several minutes—our own personal version of "Waterloo."

I'm not sure how she knew. But Miss Kenny knew we were playing in the water. Even though it wasn't written in her lesson plans for the day, she decided to teach us an important lesson. She did something I would never have expected. She opened the bathroom door.

She walked in! Miss Kenny—a girl—walked into the boys' bathroom. I didn't care that we had been caught. I didn't mind being soaked. I didn't even notice that we had sprayed water all over the tile, walls, and mirrors. My only sense of mortification focused on Miss Kenny standing there, arms folded, tapping her foot in one of several small puddles on the floor. I could not believe my eyes. Was there no place for privacy? The sign on the door said in plain English, "Boys," and yet there she stood.

Embarrassed at the sight of Miss Kenny standing there next to the urinals, I turned my crimson face toward the door and joined my fellow combatants in a forced march back to our classroom, back to corporal punishment. Back to my seat in front of Debbie Spengler and the laughter of every girl in class who saw Miss Kenny open the boys' bathroom door and walk in. I found it difficult to "sit tall." I felt two inches high, and besides that, the "ruler" had spoken.

I still remember what I learned that day, though. On one level, I learned that if I ever got in a water fight in the school bathroom, someone I least expected could walk in on me. (Even after all these years, I still never play in the water in the bathroom!) But on a deeper level, without even knowing it, Miss Kenny taught me there is no such thing as a secret place to hide and play games. I've seen it over and over again. He knows. The Master Teacher stands at every secret door, and when he hears the childish noise, he walks into the room of my childish ways. He responds. He just can't resist the opportunity to teach us a better way to live. It's always been that way with him. It's always been that way with the Master Teacher.

Day after day, crowds learned from him, the Master Teacher teaching about the kingdom. The teacher used language they could understand. He introduced the idea that God was our Father "who art in heaven." Success in kingdom life consisted of simply obeying, becoming like a child. Most of the time he didn't lay down the law; he fulfilled it. Sometimes, he taught them by telling them stories—faith and a tiny mustard seed, a light under a basket, a pearl lost, a prodigal son found. He taught that wise men build houses on rocks; foolish men build on sand. He mentioned the Samaritans; they aren't all bad apples. And then, to prove it, he told them a story about a good one.

Some days he didn't use stories; he just laid truth on the line. On one particularly inspiring day, he took a walk up a hill of learning. The teacher climbed to a higher venue, an appropriate place to teach people a loftier level of living. The crowd followed him, but they weren't looking for fancy philosophies. They needed something that would stick to the ribs of their souls. Probably a lot like you and me, they were desperate to hear something that would help them get a grip. And so, the Radical One challenged them to the climb of their lives. He looked them straight in the face, and began to teach them.

And this is what he said:[1]

To "hangers on"—those who were poverty-stricken of spirit and barely managing to cope with life on the edge—he didn't say, "You poor things. There, there." No, he said:

"You're blessed when you're at the end of your rope. With less of you, there is more of God and his rule."

To tough guys who never cry—the folks who can't admit how sad they really are—he didn't say, "Tough it out; be independent. Never let 'em see you sweat!" No, he said:

"You're blessed when you feel you've lost what is most dear to you. Only then can you be embraced by the One most dear to you."

To those troubled souls—the ones who notice that everyone else seemed to get all the talent—he didn't say, "Stick with me, and you'll be famous; the new you is just around the corner; follow the Yellow Brick Road until you meet the Wizard of Oz." Instead, he said:

"You're blessed when you're content with just who you are—no more, no less. That's the moment you find yourselves proud owners of everything that can't be bought."

And to those with a "wait" problem—those impatient and always hungry for satisfaction—he didn't say, "If you walk with me, there'll be a chicken in every pot, a sumptuous, fair life." Instead, he answered:

"You're blessed when you've worked up a good appetite for God. He's food and drink in the best meal you'll ever eat."

To the stingy souls—those too wrapped up in their own packing to give much thought to reaching out to others—he didn't say, "Take care of *numero uno;* if you don't, no one else will." Instead, he said:

"You're blessed when you care. At the moment of being care-full, you will find yourselves cared for."

To secretive men who act like little boys—those whose lives on the outside belie their aloneness and sin on the inside—he didn't say, "What happens behind the closed doors of your life is nobody's business but your own." Instead, he said:

"You're blessed when you get your inside world—your mind and heart—put right. Then you can see God in the outside world."

To pushy people—those who have a hard time keeping their hurtful thoughts and words to themselves—he didn't say, "It's a jungle out there; do unto others before they do unto you." Rather, he said:

"You're blessed when you can show people how to cooperate instead of compete or fight. That's when you discover who you really are and your place in God's family."

And finally, to those who decide to commit to The Climb—to those with guts to follow this New and Living Way—he doesn't say, "You've just bought a house on easy street. Watch me, while I demonstrate how to achieve popularity and fun in ten easy steps." Instead, he challenged those who would follow him to an incredible adventure, one so demanding it's a matter of life and death. He offered no games to play, no doors to hide behind. Instead:

"In order to live, you've got to die."

"In order to gain, you've got to lose."

"If you want to learn to 'sit tall,' go stand in the back of the line."

"If you want to be the greatest, learn and embrace servanthood."

No wonder people walked off that hillside shaking their heads. Undeniable truth had come, the Master Teacher had begun class. God Become Flesh had told them not to worry, to seek the kingdom of God first, and everything else would fall into place. Here was radical teaching, but . . .

If what he said was true, then nothing else mattered.

And if what he said wasn't the truth, well then . . . nothing else mattered anyway.

5

Passion

When I met my Randee for the first time, I had just arrived in California to start college. I must confess that one of the driving forces behind my selection of a college on the West Coast had nothing to do with what I sensed about divine direction, but rather a curiosity: I wanted to see some of the world, and more particularly, I wanted to see the ocean. A short distance from where I grew up, the mighty Mississippi runs a mile wide. It's a great river, but not an ocean. And bizarre as it may sound, I chose a school in California because I wanted to see and experience the Pacific Ocean.

The college I attended was south of San Jose, nestled in the beautiful California redwoods, but it was still several miles from the coast. On the very first day I arrived on campus, after I got settled in, I drove to Santa Cruz, a coastal community on the Monterey Bay.

My first sight of the sea mesmerized me. Even after all these years, I can still taste it with my memory. The air smelled dank and heavy with salt, and the lid of gray fog that hung over the bay made the day damp and wet as a pot of cool steam. The seagulls above the shore looked like gliders riding the wind's updrafts, their bodies white and silent as falling feathers. Fishing boats of every ilk and kind bobbed on the waters. People fished off the pier, looking like ships at anchor, tethered to the sea by baited hooks, poles, and lines. The Pacific Ocean was better than I had imagined. More beautiful and romantic than I had expected.

It didn't take me long; within the first few hours of coming to California, I fell in love with the sea.

That first evening in "paradise," I went to an arcade on the boardwalk in Santa Cruz with some guys from our campus. We met other students from the college who were also there; Randee was among them. She told me later that on that first evening when we were introduced, I played a pinball machine for nearly twenty minutes and hardly looked up to say hello. I don't remember that, but Randee does. And she's reminded me often that when we first met, it wasn't love at first sight.

But it didn't take me long.

Within a few days of my arrival on campus, Randee and I started having lunch together in the cafeteria. Not great food, but scintillating conversation. At first, we just visited and commiserated about classes we were taking or some test we had just bombed. But soon, my notice of her heart and sensitive spirit caused me to look deeper into her wonderful green eyes.

The smell of cafeteria food often drove Randee and me to seek other places to talk. One of our favorite destinations was back to the sea, back to the morning fog, and perhaps . . . back to the future. We walked along the beaches and let the cold Pacific waters freeze our feet. And as we walked, we talked.

We mused about music and travel and books. We talked of God and our mutual calls to full-time ministry. We discussed deep and abiding things—aspirations, doubts, fears, challenges, hopes, and dreams. We exchanged childhood memories. We sat for hours in coffee shops and emptied our wallets of all the photographs of our relatives, talking about each one, describing how wonderful roots and heritage can be. I went home with her on weekends and got acquainted with her family—her mom and dad, her sisters and brothers.

Yes, she had become my confidant and friend. And before many weeks had passed, I knew. I came to an understanding, a certain knowing. The process of our meeting and the depth and development of our relationship compelled me. Life without Randee seemed an unacceptable option. Whatever it took to convince her. Whatever it took to be with her. I fell in love with this girl. And within four months of meeting Randee, I did a weighty and serious thing.

I proposed. I asked her to be my wife.

And she said, "Yes."

And we became engaged. We're still engaged.

I'm positive we're engaged, because I looked that word up this morning, in two separate sources. First, I checked my *Clear and Simple Thesaurus Dictionary* by Grosset and Dunlap. I read that *engaged* means "involved . . . entangled . . . absorbed . . . engrossed . . . promised . . . committed." That was us, all right. And that *is* us. Through all of the perseverance and growth and change of our marriage relationship over the years, *engaged* represents most closely what we are about. Not perfect. Not even necessarily ideal. Just involved, entangled, absorbed, engrossed, promised . . . committed.

But just to make sure I had it right, I checked the definitive source, the Bible (God). It's there, all right—his word for *engaged*. You'll find it in the section about the day he went to the sea in search of the bride.

As the sun made its way across the morning sky that day, the Son walked along the Sea of Galilee. The angels pressed their noses against the windows of heaven to watch him. They were sure he did not journey to these shores out of any mere sense of curiosity or the fascination of seeing a body of water wider than the Jordan River. The hosts of heaven had already learned from watching him. He never took a step without purpose and plan. The angels suspected that this day would be no different.

They were right. He wasn't just "out to see the world." He was out to save it.

"Where is he going, holy Lord?" they asked the Father.

And the Father of all replied, "He is going to meet his prospective bride." Initially, the angel chorus must have broken out in song that morning at the thought of a heavenly wedding and a royal bride. This was wonderful news, and they peeked over the portals of heaven to get a better view. They could hardly wait to see this fortunate soul, this bride-to-be. They did not know who could possibly meet the qualifications and expectations of God Almighty and the Prince of heaven.

And so, they questioned among themselves, "Where will the Prince find his bride?" Of course, the God of heaven heard their questions, but he did not answer. Instead, he decided to let them learn for themselves.

The angels wondered at the menagerie of people following the Prince, listening to what he had to say. All they saw were hapless people, an arcade of people locked into the games they played, desperate ones who rarely looked up from their busyness. Unkempt souls everywhere the angels looked, but still no sign of a beautiful bride. As their keen eyes surveyed the land and the shoreline, all they could see were fishing boats and people. But now, they noticed something—a remarkable similarity. They had never observed before how much fishing boats and people seemed alike.

"Look, Sovereign," one of them mentioned. "Empty vessels. The boats and the people are both empty vessels." (Angels, though not all-knowing or powerful like their Master, show keen insight into men at times.)

And God nodded an all-knowing nod. Empty, indeed. Boats hollow and unoccupied, moored in the shallows after a disappointing night of fishing. And people, empty hulls, windless lives devoid of meaningful life and desperately alone.

"Which one, Lord?" the angels asked. "Which one of these does he love?"

And the Father answered, "All of them. He loves them all . . . one at a time."

The angels continued to watch intently now, as the master of the wind and waves climbed into the empty boat of a man named Simon and began to teach the people. But he did more than just climb into a man's boat; he climbed into his life. He engaged Simon in such an incredible conversation that day that nothing in his life would ever be the same. He gave him a fishing lesson; he taught him how to catch fish. But he also gave him a new name: Peter. He proposed a challenge to a real hardhead, a rock of a man. "Follow me," he said, "and I'll make you a fisher of men."

And so the courtship began. Fishermen left their boats behind. Groups of people walked away from their meaningless lives and began to follow him. Life apart from Jesus was no longer a viable option for them. In the days that followed, they sat and talked with him by the hour. They listened to him describe life in the kingdom. Day after day, he expressed the evidence of his love for them, sight for the blind and hearing for the deaf. In his presence they found forgiveness and hope and healing. They were individuals whom he chose and loved, one at a time. In every sense of the word, he proposed marriage to his bride, and demonstrated his engagement by becoming involved, entangled, absorbed, engrossed, promised, committed . . . forever.

Nothing has changed. He still chooses us one at a time. He still changes us one heart at a time.

We have been spoken for, and we need to start acting like it. The commitment he shows we must show.

But many of us tire of the work of commitment; we tire of The Climb. Church research specialist George Barna once declared that the number-one discouragement for pastors in America today is a lack of commitment on the part of the laity. That doesn't surprise me. It's too easy for people to switch churches. Too easy for us to stay at home and not go to church at all. Very difficult to get people excited about spiritual things. Our temporal, "throw-away" society has spawned a generation of passionless people.

I don't believe people want to be uncommitted. To the contrary, movements like Promise Keepers underscore the hunger in the hearts of people for a renewed passion and commitment. But the fact remains: The passionless Christian is an all-too-common occurrence in the church today. Such people, devoid of passion, cannot stay long on The Climb.

In all honesty, as I write this book there are days when describing commitment to The Climb challenges my vocabulary. But I did think of one word that seemed to fit, one word that might help point the way back to our First Love—*engaged*. Even though Christ chose us as his bride, we are still engaged to him, and understanding that will remind us of his commitment to us and our need for a daily relationship. We are to be "involved . . . entangled . . . and promised." Forever!

A promise has been entered into between God and man. And the mystery of it all must never be forgotten (see Eph. 5:32). Maybe in the final analysis, that's what's wrong with the world.

Maybe that's an area for growth in the church as well. Too many people who remember when they got married . . . but somewhere along the route and The Climb, forgot they're still engaged.

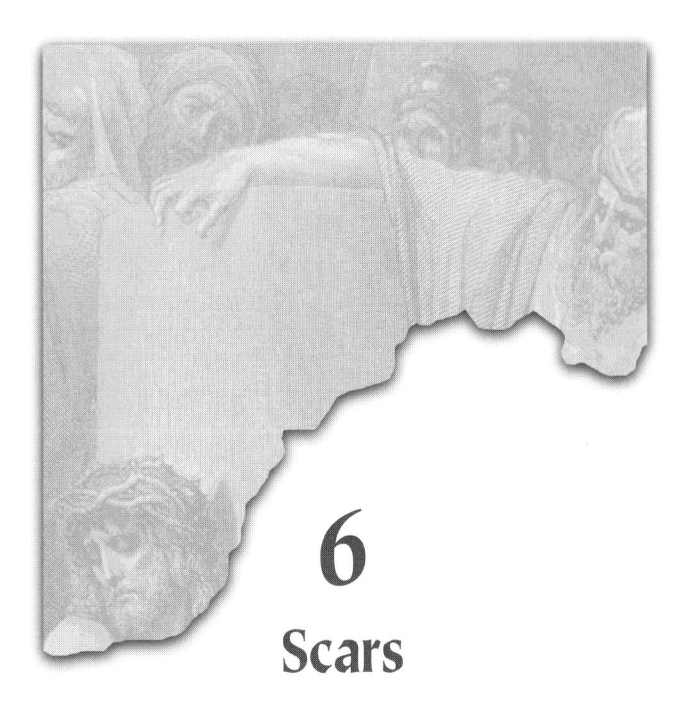

6
Scars

When I die, they'll never find them all. Even if they do an autopsy. Even if they carefully scan the topography of this well-worn, fleshly shroud called "me," they won't find them all—those off-white lines in my flesh, some straight, some jagged. I have a zillion scars. They serve as mile-markers in my life. They chronicle events and momentous happenings along the way, reminders of the road toward maturity. They represent medals won in the pain of the trek, reminders of the hazardous nature of The Climb.

One faint scar rests in the palm of my right hand; I got it when I was about ten, while throwing a knife at an old garage door. The knife didn't stick. At least, not in the garage door. It bounced straight back at my head, and I have a scar in my right palm to prove that the hand is quicker than the eye. I have three scars on my left hand, too, all of them created on the same day—the day I helped my dad cut and nail some birds-eye maple flooring in a church foyer. Maple flooring wears like iron; it saws like iron, too. As I tried to cut a short piece of it for my dad, the handsaw I held slipped out of the board I was cutting and ripped across the exposed flesh of my left hand and fingers. Excruciating pain. Exquisite scars.

I have various other dents and dings in my carcass, skin that's been scraped, knees that have had the hide knocked off more than once. A large birthmark roughly the shape of South America spreads across half of my back. Even that birthmark has its own, personal scar. When I was a teenager, my cousin Billy Chilton tried to throw a firecracker over my head on the Fourth of July. The wind caught that firecracker, and the subsequent explosion blew an uneven crater in my map of South America, just about where Rio de Janeiro would be.

Of course, some scars are more involved and more elusive, more difficult to identify.

One summer day, as I played catch in our backyard with my cousin Terry Kofahl, I casually turned my head to ask my dad a question. At that same, unfortunate moment, Terry fired me one of his best fastballs. I turned my head back toward him just in time to catch it squarely in the left eye, proving that the hand is not always quicker than the eye. A knot swelled almost instantly on my face, a purple mound the size of a golf ball. The pitch nearly knocked me unconscious. It scared everyone around me, but I wasn't too worried. After a few days, the swelling subsided; the abrasion healed. Not even a scar.

At least not on the outside.

But inside my head, above the orbital lobe of my left eye, the blow had caused a tumor to begin to develop. It grew slowly, silently for almost six years until it reached a size that affected my eyesight. I didn't even realize it was there until I went to my ophthalmologist for a change in my glasses. He discovered the tumor. A rare form of benign tumor had been growing for a long time. About the size of your thumb, it had been undetected for years, hidden from sight in the orbital lobe.

They operated and removed that growth. I still have the scar to prove it. A hairline mark just above my left eye. But you'd have to know it was there to find it; it's virtually invisible, tucked in the fold of the lid.

My guess is that as you've been reading about my scars, your mind has let you travel back in time to think about your own. Scars are a little bit like babies, I think. Once you bring up the subject, everyone has a unique story to tell. The next time you're in a group of people, ask one of them to share the story of their first child's birth. Just start talking about birthing babies and watch what happens. Details about the perturbations of labor soon follow: dilation, breathing, pushing, pain. Doctors hurrying in to deliver the baby (or not showing up at all). How long the labor lasted. How much the baby weighed. Everyone has a story about the day the twins were born, or the race to the hospital in the snowstorm the day baby what's-his-name came along.

And everyone has a story about scars, too.

Everyone can point to scars on their shins, or the gravel marks still embedded in their knees from the time they fell on the parking lot in the fifth grade. Most of us can remember how many stitches it took to close the cut we got when we stepped on the glass at the beach, or ripped our arm on a nail.

But some scars suggest more than a temporary and cosmetic discomfort. They permanently mark the landscape of lives touched by tragedy. Burns. Birth defects. Car accidents. They all possess tremendous potential for scarring lives, marking our lives with lasting pain, and often lasting consequences.

All of these sorrows disfigure and leave scars, some of them ugly and embarrassing. Some of those scars are obvious to all who pass by. Other scars, however, like divorce or abuse, run deep and dark, dark as any secret cave, and hidden from human view. Those scars don't cause us to talk; they cause us to want to hide, to give up, to lose heart in the midst of The Climb.

But they do not escape the Master's sight. He sees them all, and knows of their origins and purposes. Read on, and you will see two lives, two weary souls, trapped and discouraged in The Climb, scarred by the blades of life . . . and touched by the Balm of Gilead.

Love Letters in the Sand

Before daybreak, he began to stir. The angels of heaven must have watched the Sovereign all night long as he prayed and then rested on the Mount of Olives. But now, he awoke and readied himself for a day in the temple courts. Like a man on a mission, like a teacher preparing for the classes of the day, he must have prepared his mind and heart. He began the climb down the hillside, committed to the day and ministry ahead.

Across town, at that moment, in a private residence, a woman rolled over in her warm bed, a borrowed bed and not her own. The dark night would soon give way to morning's light. She covered her head with the blanket, coveting a few more moments of slumber before she must get up. But she was not alone. She slept with a man. And the man with whom she shared this rumpled bed was not her husband. She must leave before the dawn; she must leave before the light of day could expose her naked and adulterous shame. A rooster crowed, breaking the vial of morning stillness, but her sleep remained deep and sound.

Just at dawn, the Teacher found his way into the temple courts. He loved these walls; he loved these people who came each day to hear him talk and teach and tell of the Father's kingdom. Even at this early hour, they eagerly sought him out; he sat down in their midst, and they gathered around him to listen.

The sleepy one in the borrowed bed was not there in the temple, of course. But she would be soon. For at about the time Jesus sat down to teach, several teachers of the law and the Pharisees broke the vile stillness of her sleep and slumber by entering the house where she slept. One of them must have been watching that night to know firsthand of her indiscretion. Jewish law required more than compromising circumstances. Witnesses must have seen the accused sinner engaged in the sex act. Apparently someone had watched. And now the teachers and Pharisees dragged her from her bed of shame. Time for the law to take its course. Time to go to the temple and expose her scar to all.

And so it was that divine providence introduced Christ the Innocent to a woman caught in adultery. I cannot help but wonder about the expressions on the faces of those "spiritual men" as they brought the shamed and shameless woman before him. For a certainty, they knew their actions would bring humiliation and disgrace upon the woman, as they forced her to stand before all of the people in the temple courts.

But what of him? Did they seek to embarrass him, this bachelor teacher who had never "known" a woman? Did they hope her scandalous acts, described and outlined in this public hearing, would so confuse and unsettle him that he would not know how to answer their hard and stony question? I do not know. I only know they sought to trap him, hoping his answer would give them license for accusation.

They pushed the woman to the front of the crowd and then beyond, into the clearing. Behind her stood a wall of accusers, pointing fingers aimed at her reputation. But in front of her, she was surrounded by Love.

"Caught in the act," they announced to the Teacher. "The law says crush her skull with rocks. So . . . what do you say?"

Alone now, the woman stood silent as a lamb, silent before the Lamb, mute and stoic, a hard and distant expression chiseled into her countenance. I imagine that the shame of this moment, the shame of her life, might have caused her gaze to focus on the ground. She could not look her accusers in the face, and so with head bowed, hands at her sides, she looked down.

Down toward the dirt at her feet.

Down, like the scum of the earth.

Jesus said nothing, nothing at all. Instead, he stooped and began to write on the ground.

Their querying continued; their plot to trap him had been set. They would not be appeased by his silence. The law demanded judgment. The law demanded an answer.

And so, he did answer them. He straightened up and addressed them: "If you are sinless, you go first. Throw the first rock, if you dare." Then he stooped again to continue his writing on the ground. Divine hand touching the scum of the earth. He began to write on the ground. The same finger that etched the law in tablets of stone for Moses now inscribed a message of grace for a woman familiar with shame.

The accusers stood silent at first. Then one by one they began to walk away. The old ones left first; perhaps they were the first to realize their own hypocrisy. But eventually, even the younger ones dropped the aspersions they cast and the stones they were about to throw, and silently walked away.

Finally, just the two of them: the shamed woman and the sinless man. The two who had started the morning in such different circumstances faced each other in the middle of the temple courts.

"Where are they?" he asked her. "Has no one condemned you?"

"No one, sir," she answered.

"Then, neither do I. Go, and leave your life of sin," said the Master.

Where did she go after this incredible moment with him? Did she turn her life around? Did she choose to follow him? The Scriptures do not indicate. Perhaps the scars of her past and the bitterness of her shame so mortally wounded her that she would not mend her ways. But I do not believe that was so.

I believe she committed to The Climb; I believe she decided to leave the darkness of her sinful and embedded ways and follow him. I believe there must have been a day when she told her story to a fellow climber, some fellow traveler wounded from the stones people throw, wearied and bludgeoned from accusations and failures.

"Hold on," she must have said. "Your wounds can be healed; your shame is not so grievous that it is beyond hope." I believe at that moment, she showed the other traveler her life with its faint scars. Hairline reminders of past pain, they were barely visible and thin as wispy lines drawn in the sand of time.

And when that traveler asked her from whence the scars came, I believe she disclosed a deep and profound secret for mending broken lives. I think the once-adulterous woman told the other traveler what he wrote on the ground that day.

Many scholars have speculated about the content of the message he wrote in the dirt with his finger. No one but the people standing in the temple courts that day knows for sure, of course. But I do have an opinion. I believe he wrote a letter, a scarlet letter, with words red as blood. I believe he wrote a message of love and forgiveness in the dirt of this world. The finger of God wrote a crimson message that contained eternal truth, and around her life's failures his fingers had sutured and sewn tight grace and wholeness. He had healed her. And now she accepted his handwritten invitation to join The Climb.

House Call

She was not the first, of course. He touched and healed many scars before hers. Several weeks earlier he had strolled through Jerusalem.

Jerusalem. I cannot help but wonder what it was like for Jesus to climb those steps into the holy city of David. He who created every star and planet now walked those streets where Kings David and Solomon once ruled. Like an artist who paints a landscape replete with characters and is then somehow able to enter the scene he has just painted, God Become Flesh moved into the everyday-ness of mere men and walked among them.

On this particular day, The Climb led up to Jerusalem for a feast of the Jews. In lockstep with the Father's plan, he made his way through the city streets, like hundreds of other young Jewish males of his day.

Just north of the temple area, near the Sheep Gate, five colonnades surrounded a pool of water called Bethesda, which means *house of healing*. But more than covered colonnades surrounded the pool. There were people. Hordes of people gathered every day to beg and plead for alms. Scarred people. The physically disabled—the blind, lame, and paralyzed—gathered around this pitiful pool every day hoping someone would have mercy on their plight.

What did he see? As the humble servant walked among those weary and heavy laden of life, what did he really see? Perhaps he saw the dirt on unwashed faces. Maybe he noticed the unkempt appearance of people unable to care for their own basic needs because arms hung useless at their sides, limp as willow limbs.

What did he smell? Was the odor pungent and overwhelming as he moved among them, listening to their calls for help? Some of the disabled probably rarely bathed because of the extraordinary effort it took for them to get into the pool. And what of those who could not see? What did he think of them? What was it like for them? Did they notice the shadow of the Light of Day who passed among them? Did they notice the Son's presence as their blind eyes glazed toward his countenance, eyes that had never known the light, scaled eyes, scarred, and covered, dark and dusky as a total eclipse at midday?

We do not know what he saw or heard or smelled. We only know that he walked there among them, in the midst of their world . . . and his own.

But perhaps the most important question to ask is, What did he say? What could anyone say in the midst of such misery and human suffering? What could he say that would allay their pain? Perhaps the challenge to climb would ring hollow in the ears of these who could not hear or see or walk.

As Jesus made his way through the crowd, he came upon one particular soul, crippled and lying on his mat. Jesus knew—a certain knowing impressed him. He knew the scarred man had been lame for thirty-eight long years, unable to move about as other men, his legs useless limbs connected to an otherwise healthy trunk. Jesus examined the man with his eyes, like a doctor making his morning rounds. No need to explain. No need to bring the Great Physician up to speed on this patient's medical history. He already knew. Omniscience always knows what's wrong.

But Jesus did ask one question for information's sake. He asked a question that I believe the cripple had never been asked before: "Do you want to get well?"

But the man did not answer Jesus' question. When Jesus asked the man whether he wanted to be well, the man simply told Jesus why he was lame: "There's nobody to help me in the pool."

The superstition of that day said that once a year an angel would come to stir the waters of the pool. If you happened to be the first one into the pool after that event, then supposedly you would be healed. But the Bible doesn't support that old superstition. I don't believe there ever were any angels who came and stirred the pool. And the people who gathered there day after day hoped for something hopeless—an angel who would never come.

You probably know the rest of the story; if not, check it out for yourself in the Gospel of John, chapter five. Jesus told the man to take his mat and go. He told a crippled man straight to his face to climb off his pitiful bedroll, fold it up, and walk. He healed the man.

Great story.

Great ending.

But still, that puzzling question that was never really answered: "Do you want to get well?" What kind of question was that? Wasn't the answer obvious? Wouldn't anyone want to get well if they had been crippled for thirty-eight years? Wouldn't anyone jump at the chance to trade in their bum legs for an opportunity to join The Climb and follow him?

Maybe.

Maybe not. Being committed to The Climb is never a matter of having the strength or limbs for the ascent, but rather the desire to turn around. Remember? A little later in that same fifth chapter of John, Jesus bumps into the man at the temple, and tells him to stop sinning, ". . . or something worse may happen to you" (verse 14).

Sinning? What sinning? You might be tempted to say, "Come on, Lord. Cut the guy some slack. He's a victim of life's circumstance. It's not his fault he's been lying on a mat for thirty-eight years. How much trouble can you get into when your whole world consists of a blanket-sized mat?" Evidently, enough. Enough trouble to cripple him from the inside out. Maybe he was too complacent. Maybe life on a measured mat fit him too well. Perhaps he had become too used to giving lame excuses about an angel that wasn't ever coming, or legs that didn't work. Or he had become so accustomed to bemoaning his circumstances that he failed to realize another, even more crippling problem in his life. An "attitude" problem, sin that ran past his legs that didn't walk and permeated the bony skeleton of his soul.

The Bible doesn't specifically mention it, but I believe that the day the lame man was healed, he did more than climb out of bed; he made an "internal assent." He said yes to the question of wellness that Jesus asked. He took an inventory. He looked at his life. He looked at his world: a measured mat, with defined boundaries and limited demands. And he embraced the challenge of the Master to commit to The Climb. Time to stand up. Time to grow up, stop the sinning, and move on.

From that moment, the man could never again use empty excuses for not climbing. No more blaming others for not lending a hand. No more excuses about miracles that never came, or the angel who never showed up. Instead, he chose to get well from the inside out and change his place of residence—eternally.

The most difficult scars to deal with in life are those that refuse to be healed. I'll bet you've got some. I know I do. Open sores. Things I didn't ask for. Lumps in life that show up and then won't go away. Circumstances that make everyday living the pits, some disfiguring birthmark on your life that refuses to disappear under vanishing cream. But there are worse things than the scars of life. The saddest people in this world are not the ones with the scars that won't ever go away. The most tragic people in the world are the ones who choose not to recover from the effects of the scarring.

Being committed to The Climb never depends on strength of limb for the ascent; it demands a continual willingness to turn around, to face the

Light every day. Even in the presence of the pain of the journey, we never get permission from him to lead a lame life. He still chooses to walk into the midst of what's wrong with the picture of our lives. His Spirit still diagnoses the ailments and aches of the human heart. He knows. Omniscience always knows, and he identifies with the problems and brings his own salve and solution.

For me, then, there is but one thing remaining. I must answer the question . . . every day. Answer the haunting question, the one he asked while standing on the doorstep of the house of healing, a difficult, unavoidable, and daily query for all of us scathed and scarred in The Climb: "Do I want to get well?"

7

Friendship with God

Ask most pastors their favorite day of the week, and they would probably place Monday at the bottom. Monday is the day after Sunday. And Sunday is the day we preach, the day we teach, the day we do our best to encourage and instruct the people of God in The Climb. We who are called to pastoral ministry want to do our best every Sunday, of course. But often we come away feeling as though we could have done more, could have said it differently, could have inspired the people more effectively. Couple that reality with the rush of adrenaline that most pastors experience every Lord's Day, and the emotional hangover the morning after can be severe. I know one pastor who says he thinks about resigning every Monday.

As a pastor, I recognize the emotional drain—that's why I rarely get too involved with sticky issues on Mondays. Open the mail. Dictate a few letters. Let the batteries recharge, and get over the "adrenal downer drain" of Sunday.

But it doesn't always turn out that way.

One innocent and mellow Monday morning recently, my secretary buzzed to say I had a phone call. One of my staff pastors had a quick question, she said. After a few casual remarks, he got to the matter at hand. "Pastor, have you had any calls about Jim's adult class yesterday?"

"No," I answered, but a feeling deep inside my Monday-morning gut told me I was about to. Something was said in one of our adult education classes the previous day, and my staff associate didn't want me to get blindsided with it. The teacher, who had many years of experience in teaching adult Bible studies, gave his class of eighty students a rather disturbing bit of spiritual trivia to ponder for the next week's class: "Before we go," he said, "I want you to think this week about one important fact: God is not your friend."

And then he closed in prayer.

And then the people left the class and went home to think.

And then my phone started to ring.

I received five or six calls that morning, all of them slight variations on the same theme. More or less, the folks who called wanted to lynch the teacher. He might as well have said that the King James Bible wasn't holy or that the Revised Standard Version wasn't all that revised. "Pastor, in class on Sunday, Jim said God wasn't our friend. You weren't there, but several of us were very upset. How could someone stand and say God isn't our friend, when the Bible so clearly teaches us that he *is* our friend?" They looked to me for a clarifying answer, a theological position. They looked to me to tell them what *we* believed.

Well, I didn't bite. I refused to play the role of the Bible "answer man." Instead, I responded with a question of my own: "What makes you think God is your friend?"

"Isn't he?" they would reply. "I thought the Bible said, 'There is a friend that sticketh closer than a brother.' Doesn't it say that?"

I would answer, "Yes, I believe the Bible says that."

"And doesn't the Bible say that Jesus called his disciples 'friends'?" they asked.

Again, my answer: "Yes, I believe the Bible says that."

"Then why don't you believe we are God's friend?" they would question.

And then I would answer them, "I do. I do believe we are God's friend, but that is not the same as God being our friend."

I had some great conversations that day with some wonderful people. I still haven't changed my mind, though. God has no need of our friendship. He doesn't want to be our friend; he wants to be our Lord, our God. The difference between my being God's friend and his being my friend is the difference between finding a "bosom buddy" and being found in the bosom of God. It's the difference between . . . well, heaven and earth. Light years separate the two ideas. When God spoke of Abraham, he called him friend (Isa. 41:8). But when Abraham spoke of God, he called him God Most High, Creator of heaven and earth, sovereign Lord (Gen. 14:22; 15:2). He did not call him friend.

It's not, of course, such a terrible thing to call Jesus our friend. Perhaps most Christians do. I believe that those first climbing companions of Jesus—all twelve of them—viewed him as their friend. In fact, I think they looked at each other as friends, too. They called each other by name. The twelve of them must have felt like brothers as they followed their friend Jesus around the countryside watching his miracles and listening to his teaching. They must have all felt fortunate to be so close to the Master. And yet, even though a true bonding and friendship must have developed between all of them, there were moments of honest disagreement among friends, times when sibling rivalry among the brethren had to be addressed.

One day Jesus took his friends—the Twelve—aside for a chat. And the angels of heaven watched and were glad.

"Look," one of them said. "The Son is talking to his friends. See how they sit and listen to him. See how intimate their friendship grows." But this conversation between Jesus and his climbing companions ran deeper than an idle stream of thought. Once more, the Lamb spoke of suffering and death. As the angels listened, they were saddened by what they heard the Sovereign say.

"We are going up to Jerusalem," said the Prince of Peace. And he described an awful scene. The Son of Man . . . betrayed; the chief priests and teachers of the law condemn him to death and hand him over to the Gentiles. The pagans mock him . . . spit on him . . . flog him . . . kill him! Three days dead . . . then alive!

The angels sat in stunned silence. The horror of it all. How could people treat the Sovereign with such contempt? How could they miss God's obvious expression of love?

Jesus' friends, the disciples, sat and listened without emotion. One of the angels who watched spoke up. "They will know how to console him. One of the Twelve will know what to say to bring comfort to the Lamb." And so the angels watched and waited to see what would happen next with Jesus and his friends.

Well, nothing happened, nothing at all. Not one of the Twelve moved to comfort the Lamb. Not one of his friends came alongside. No one said, "This is tragic news. This must not be. What succor and solace can we bring?" Instead, every man sat silent as falling snow, mute and still. They looked as if they had no understanding of the profoundness of what had just been said.

The angels looked away. They turned their faces toward the Father, knowing he watched it all.

But then . . . a stirring among the ranks of the Twelve.

James and John stood, almost in unison, and walked to a woman nearby, their mother. They whispered something to her, perhaps a secret. The other disciples weren't sure what the clandestine meeting was about. But they watched as she took her boys and walked over to Jesus. She kneeled in his presence.

"Finally," said one of the angels. "At last, someone comes to comfort and encourage the Master." And they listened for what she would say.

But the woman did not kneel at his feet bringing a balm of comfort. Instead, she entreated him for a favor. She asked the Master for the choicest seats in the kingdom. In one sense, not a selfish appeal. She did not ask for herself. She knelt in humility, making the request for her sons. And now, the two mama's boys spoke up. Yes, they would like to sit next to him on his throne—one on the right, and one on the left.

They didn't know what they asked for. These two progeny, standing behind their mother's skirt, didn't understand.

"What of the cup I'm about to drink? Could you embrace that cup, bitter as gall?" he asked.

"Of course we can drink out of that cup," they answered. Maybe they were so sure of themselves because they had shared the same cup with him so many times before.

Friends who had shared in so much, seen so much. Mature friends, they were. Men ready to enlist. Committed to The Climb and asking a favor. And if they needed a stiff drink from a bitter cup, bring it on. They were ready.

"Yes. Yes, you will indeed drink from my cup," said Jesus. But the seats weren't his to give away. The Father had reserved them; he would handle the seating arrangements.

And now, another commotion. The other ten followers had caught wind of what was happening. Like jealous playground children, they surrounded the two brothers. Their selfish hearts welled with indignation at the thought that these two would try to get the choicest seats in the kingdom.

I wonder who spoke up first. Perhaps it was Judas, the thief, who first broke the steely silence. "Not fair!" he might have said. "How dare you try to steal the influence. I'm the one who handles the money. It's only right that I sit closest to the King." Or perhaps Thomas spoke first. "I'm not surprised you two tried this sort of stunt," he might have said. "Blood's thicker than water. I've doubted your loyalty to the rest of us from the beginning." Or perhaps Peter. The hardhead. The big mouth. The one who walked on water with Jesus but soon would walk away. Maybe he was the first to push his way to the front and demand that these two opportunists back off and give way.

We do not know who spoke first. We only know who spoke last.

Twelve grown men acted like children, pushing, shoving, and elbowing each other for the front of the line. They jostled for position as one lowly servant spoke to them about greatness. A dozen men raised their hands and begged, "Pick me, Teacher, pick me!" and Jesus answered quietly with a word of instruction. In essence, he said that greatness in the kingdom does not depend on games people play but their willingness to follow the leader.

"Whoever wants to become great among you must be your servant," he said. To commit to The Climb, their friend and leader said, is to march toward the cheap seats, the lowly place of servanthood and slavery and dying to self. A very expensive proposition, indeed.

"And whoever wants to be first must be your slave," said the Master.

Were they disappointed in his answer? Probably. They all wanted to receive a special favor from their friend Jesus. But dying to self and becoming servants wasn't exactly the kind of "special treatment" they had in mind. After the Master spoke to them, they must have come to the conclusion that getting "chummy" with God was going to be more difficult than they had first imagined.

Friends of God are friends of the lowly servant, Jesus. Our friendship with God never depends on favoritism or position; it's never been a matter of *our* being special. It depends totally on *his* being special, the eternal, sovereign God who came as a suffering servant to demonstrate his love. I choose my own friends, but I didn't choose him. He chose me, and it will forever be that way.

In the final analysis, God will never be my pal. He will forever be my sovereign Lord. And The Climb is never a matter of getting close enough to God to ask him for a favor. It's a matter of staying close enough to God to *find* his favor.

We can be friends with God's Son, but if we are, it's because we please him by obeying him. As Jesus the Master has said, "You are my friends if you do what I command" (John 15:14).

8

The Mountain of Learning

Calgary sits at the edge of the Canadian Rockies. Most people have heard of its annual "Stampede." A cowboy town to some, perhaps, but when Randee and I vacationed there in the spring of 1988, we knew the city as the site of the recently held Winter Olympic games. We toured all the Olympic venues: cross-country skiing, downhill racing, even the jumping events. But nothing interested me more than the "mountain" that was the site of the luge and bobsled competition.

This was not a God-made mountain. It was man-made and not very tall. In fact, it may have been less than a few hundred feet in elevation, but the undulations of the winding tube that comprised the track for the luge and bobsled twisted and turned all the way to the bottom. One of the attendants at the visitor information center mentioned that it was too bad we weren't there on the weekend, because on the weekends they opened the luge course to the public. For twenty-five bucks you could take a luge ride down the bobsled run. I knew I had to try it.

We came back the following Saturday and arrived in the parking lot early, so I could be one of the first in line. I didn't want to take a chance on them running out of tickets. I stood waiting with several other people who all looked as intrigued and nervous as I felt. The entrance gate finally opened, and I walked to the counter and paid my money.

The nice man waiting on me at the counter glanced at me with a somewhat compassionate look as he gave me an agreement paper to sign. I don't remember all of it, but some of it read, "What you are about to do is crazy and very dangerous. You may kill your stupid self trying to act like an Olympic athlete. If that happens, don't blame us. Sign at the bottom if you promise not to hold us responsible. It's your own dumb fault!" That, of course, is a loose translation, but you get the idea. I signed the paper, and thanked the man for his compassion.

My next hint that this climb might be a little bit harrowing came with the gear they handed out at the counter: knee pads, elbow pads, and perhaps most disturbing of all, a helmet with a chin strap. Also, a luge, which, in case you've forgotten, is a sled only slightly larger than a briefcase and just barely big enough for one person. (In my case, not quite big enough for one. I could tell just by looking at my little luge that I'd hang off both sides and both ends.)

The one thing lacking in all the paraphernalia they handed across the counter was instructions on how to successfully navigate the luge course. Yet that didn't scare me; I knew someone would show us what to do or give us some directions before we actually made our "run."

Besides, I told myself, *I'm a visual learner anyway.* After I donned the protective pads and pried my head into my helmet, I began my trek to the top of the man-made peak, carrying my luge under my arm like it was an oversized box of cornflakes. Two other people in front of me marched in similar cadence. As we walked, the guy in front asked me if I had received any instructions on "how to do this!"

"No, but I'm sure they'll spend some time showing us what to do when we get there," I answered.

Within minutes we reached the summit and formed a short line in front of the gate. I watched first one of them and then the other have a brief conversation with the woman attendant, then mount their respective luges and disappear down the icy slope.

That's it? I thought. *No formal instruction? No practice or someone to demonstrate the proper technique for hurling down a sled run at one hundred miles an hour? No "how-to" video? Not even a pamphlet to read or pictures to look at?*

I felt a lump in my throat. My wife had our camera, and she snapped several pictures of me as I stood watching. She said I looked "a little pale" and asked if I was sure I wanted to do this. Of course, I was sure. I figured a person doesn't need rosy cheeks to have a cheery outlook. I'd be okay. If those other guys could do it, I could, too. So I stood my ground. I waited my turn, my face pale as paste, my luge in my gloved hands, helmet on, elbows and knees padded.

And then, it was time. Time to ride this man-made mountain. My wife hugged me and kissed me for the longest of whiles, the way she does when I go away on a long trip. She told me good-bye as if she really meant it. She said she would always love me, and it seemed to me as if "always" was a very brief period of time. Now, I stood alone at the top of that mountain.

Well, not totally alone. At the very top of the hill, that small woman employee stood waiting for me to step up and act like a man. I studied her closely as I approached. I'd been watching her for the last several minutes as she helped the two people in front of me. She didn't look old enough for such a responsible position. And now it was my turn. Too late. No turning back.

The neophyte female took my luge from me and placed it on the track. "Lie down," she said in a voice that sounded remarkably like an authoritarian Shirley Temple. As she spoke, she pointed to the narrow tube they called "the run."

"Head up; feet down," she said. Nonchalant. Not paying too much attention, as if she were loading her nine-thousandth group of tourists for the day for a ride on the Matterhorn at Disneyland. I obeyed, hoping she noticed that my luge didn't have a seat belt. I hoped against hope she would explain how to stay on this tiny piece of metal and wood all the way to end of the line. Heart already racing. On my back now, and wondering what the songwriter meant when he wrote, "Let angels prostrate fall!"

I looked up into the young woman's countenance. Her frozen gaze seemed distant and cold as the ice she pointed to. No emotion. No compassion. No word of prayer before my descent. Feet first. Hanging off both ends (and both sides) of a tiny sled.

"Stay flat, and just look over your chest to see where you're going. You steer just the way you used to when you were a kid on those snow sleds. Try not to hit the sides of the run. The cleaner your run, the faster you'll go. If you're good at it, you'll be doing twenty-five miles an hour top speed. See you at the bottom."

And with that, she took her foot and callously pushed me off. She shoved me—feet first—down a luge run I had never seen before. I didn't go ten feet before a thousand questions began to race me down the hill. I only remember the first two questions: *Why did I do this?* and *How do I stop?* Before I had a chance to try to answer myself, the first corkscrew turn slammed me into a banked angle. Frightening. Almost terrifying. My speed began to increase. Fifteen miles per hour. Twenty. Faster and faster. No brakes. No way to stop.

I may have pushed my own personal envelope of adventure too far this time, I told myself. *This might be the day I actually kill my fool self.* I felt out of control as one banked turn after another came into my sight, just over the horizon of my heaving chest and stomach as I sped down the run. (Oh, how I wished I was a little thinner, so I could have a better view of where I was heading.)

Follow directions. . . . Don't kill yourself! I thought. *This is really crazy.*

Finally, after what seemed like forty days and nights of heaving and bouncing around, the reign of terror stopped almost as quickly as it had begun. A welcome patch of sky appeared overhead. I blurred past a man at the finish line and across a piece of indoor carpet they had stretched down the run to slow the "victims" to a halt. I rolled slowly off the luge, and was tempted to kiss the carpet the way people kiss the ground when they finally get back to their own country after being hostages for a long time. Too many people watching, though, so I just tried to stand up and look brave. My weak knees wobbled a bit as I stood and walked back toward the man I had just blown past at the finish line.

"Congratulations," he said. "I think you went farther down this piece of indoor carpet than anyone we've ever had ride the luge. You must have had a totally clean run all the way to the bottom to glide this far. How was it?"

How was it? Was he kidding? It may have been a sixty-second ride, but a minute can be forever when voices inside your head keep saying, *I think I might die; I think I'm gonna die!* the entire time.

It must have been quite a scene. No ovations. No medals. No flags being hoisted while the national anthem played. Just wide-eyed me, standing there trying to recover from my much-too-rapid descent from the top of the mountain. Within moments, my wife showed up. I noticed a certain sense of surprise and relief in her voice as she kissed me and said she was really glad to see me (the way she does when I've been gone on a long trip).

If I told you the luge ride I took didn't scare the socks off me, I'd be lying. But I must also confess that I wouldn't trade the experience for anything in the world. Sometimes the greatest climbs we experience aren't memorable because of the exhilaration of the ascent but because of the incredible rush to the bottom of the run.

Some might say, "If you feared that sort of thing, why in the world did you buy your ticket? Why would you go stand in line for a chance to break your silly neck?" My response? "How would I know if I liked it or not if I never gave it a try? How would I ever know I could do it if I never gave it a shot?" I guess a part of me wants the risk, the adventure. Never pushing the edge means never pushing ahead.

It's that way with him, too. Life with the Master is an adventure. When you commit to The Climb, there will be days when, in order to obey him, you've got to let go. Hang ten. Hang it all, knowing that he's been this way before, and he'll catch you if you fall.

But don't take my word for it. Take his.

Late one afternoon, Jesus' disciples approached him about an obvious problem. The tired masses had been with the master teacher throughout the afternoon, having followed him to the top of a mountain of learning. They had continued to sit and listen as he explained the mysteries of the kingdom; they watched him heal and touch and care. These powerless people wearied of Roman bondage and they longed for Messiah to come and reign, to deliver them from the soreness of oppression. And now, as the day's shadow lengthened, their hunger and fatigue deepened.

The hungry people seemed to be camping out on the sides of the mountain. Everywhere the disciples looked, they saw men, women, and children. Thousands of them. The disciples expressed their concerns to the Master. "Send them away," they said. "The people need to get moving," they reasoned. "Bread won't mysteriously appear out of nowhere. Besides, what about the money?" The disciples could never find the funds to pay for that much food. Eight months' wages wouldn't buy enough for each person to have even one bite.

More than five thousand hungry men listened to what the Teacher would say next. Who knows how many women and children sat hoping, as well.

But he didn't send the crowd away. He sent the disciples on a mission to find out about the resources they had to work with: five small loaves, two small fish, and one willing boy, whose name is never even mentioned. More than enough for *El Shaddai*, God Almighty. For there on the mountain of learning, the mighty one taught by doing—a lesson in his power and his compassion.

The Son set a table of fish and bread and blessed it. Afterward, twelve baskets full of fragments left over, and everyone fully satisfied. Amazing, it was. In fact, so amazing that, besides the resurrection itself, this dinner party is the only miraculous sign recorded in all four Gospels.

After the meal, Jesus dismissed the multitudes and sent his disciples on ahead to the other side of the lake. He needed some time alone. Time for a climb. An opportunity to walk up a mountainside by himself to pray. We do not know the pace of his gait as he walked up that hill, but after such a long day of ministry demands and teaching, it would not be unreasonable to assume he trudged slowly toward this loft of seclusion and solitude.

The disciples boarded their boat and began to row. And as they leaned hard against the oars, pushing their vessel out into the water, the wind and the waves pushed back. Strong winds blew against the Twelve; a veritable gale forced them to an agonizingly slow pace. They must have moaned and mourned their dreadful progress. One mile. Two miles. And the night wore on like a tired old song. One o'clock. Two o'clock, the boat creeping over the surface of the deep, five yards forward, four yards back. The Twelve continued to brave the elements a considerable distance from shore.

Jesus saw the struggle of his friends and decided to walk to meet them. He left his mountainside of prayer. He walked to the water's edge, and then beyond. A casual stroll, now. It's only water. The Master of earth and sky on his way to speak to the wind and the waves. He walked into the middle of the lake.

Sometime after three in the morning, he moved into the view of his friends. They were terrified. Just the sight of such an apparition after the night of strong winds and slapping waves was enough to make grown men cry. And they did cry. They cried out in fear. They didn't recognize or expect him to come alongside them, and they just knew he was a ghost. He tried to console them. "Don't be afraid," he said. "It's me."

Then Peter decided. Peter, the impulsive one, decided to break ranks with the others. Time to bolt for the Door and escape the tossing vessel. Time to slip over the edge and risk a slippery slide down the mountainous waves.

"If it's you, Lord, tell me to come to you on the water," he said.

And then, the Word gave the word. Not a complex or compound word. Just a four-letter command. A declared imperative with nothing else added.

"Come," said the Word.

And so he did. Peter swung his legs over the side of the boat and turned the flapping sails of his soul into the wind. Too late to go back, now. Peter committed to The Climb. He got down out of the boat. He took one small step for a man and one giant leap of faith. He walked. The Bible says he actually walked on the water and began making his way toward Jesus (Matt. 14:29).

But it didn't take long. It never does when our sight walks right on past our faith. Peter noticed the wind. And he must have come to a stark realization: Almost anything is easier to get into than out of. As soon as his fear pushed him over the precipice of doubt, he began to sink like the rock he was named after.

The thrill of victory. The agony of defeat. The voice of the Master with that haunting and reasonable question: "Why did you doubt?" Jesus reached down and pulled his climbing companion out of those heaving waves. It must be true that Peter had little faith, for that is what Jesus said. And yet, I cannot help but think Peter's love for the Master and dedication to The Climb must have warmed the heart of his God. As far as we know, Peter stands alone beside the Lord Jesus as the only man who ever walked on water. Even Moses, the mighty and meek leader of Israel, needed God to part the waves. Moses and all of Israel preferred dry ground.

But there came a day—on one dark and stormy night—when the voice of Jesus and his invitation to "come" was all that was needed to catapult a rock into the mountainous waves of learning. True, he may not have skipped across the lake. He may not have danced on the surface, but he walked, didn't he? Love's compelling voice lifted him beyond himself, and the buoyancy of that moment with Light must have been incredible.

Peter had begun a short climb on his own mountain of learning. He would slip and embarrass himself as he fell along the way, no doubt. But he was willing to learn. To become a fool for God.

I wonder what the other disciples thought as they watched the two of them walking side by side on the waves. Imagine it.

Peter and Jesus, walking in faith.

Back to the safety of the boat . . .

Back to eleven men with dry feet . . .

While the wind lost its breath and died.

9

Climbing by Kneeling

Do you know where you were a year ago today? Unless it was a red-letter day like your wedding, the first day on a new job, or the birth of your child, probably not. You may have a general idea of what you were doing, or which week you went on vacation, but most of us can't recall where we were this time last year or this time two years ago. Today, as I write these words, it's January 6, and I know exactly where I was two years ago today, because it's the same place I was last year at this time.

For the last three years, I've done exactly the same thing on the first full week of the new year—

get on a bus with seventy-five or eighty other pastors and go away for four days.

Almost three years ago, God began to do something unusual in the hearts of local pastors here in Modesto, California. A hunger for prayer seemed to be continually on our minds. At a monthly luncheon of the ministerial association, the idea surfaced for having a prayer summit led by facilitators from Northwest Renewal, a ministry for the encouragement and support of pastors as they unify in prayer for their communities. We called them and asked to have an informational meeting. What we discovered was a little frightening, even for pastors (whom some people think get paid to pray). We learned that a prayer summit demands commitment, a major commitment of time. Four days of prayer. No agenda. No preachers, teachers, or seminar leaders. No videos to watch. Not even a "spiritual walk" journal to keep during the summit. Just four days of prayer.

"What's the schedule for the time together?" one pastor asked the representative. "Arrive at the conference site by noon on Monday, get checked in, have lunch, and then begin prayer by one o'clock," he said. "Pray until nearly five, before a break for dinner. Then prayer again at seven until around nine, when we celebrate communion. On Tuesday and Wednesday, breakfast at eight, prayer from nine until noon. Lunch, and then prayer from one until five. Dinner, then prayer and communion as before. Thursday, breakfast at seven-thirty and prayer from eight-thirty until nearly noon. Then load up and go home. That's the schedule."

It'll never happen, some thought. *I can't afford the time away,* others would tell themselves. But still, the pressing sense of urgency from God to come away and pray. We discussed the Northwest Renewal prayer concept at length in the ministerial steering committee, and finally we decided we would sponsor a prayer summit. We had nearly sixty pastors that first year.

I just returned from this year's summit, where seventy-seven very busy pastors walked away from their churches and responsibilities to focus on the real ministry of any saint—praying together and singing together and reading the Word together for four days. Amazing.

But something even more significant than our yearly outing has developed from the seed of our climb together to a summit of prayer. Unity. We began to feel a unity for the lost in our community unlike anything we had previously experienced. I heard speaker and author Ed Cole say once at a Promise Keepers rally that one of the by-products of prayer is intimacy. "Prayer," he said, "produces intimacy with the one *for* whom you pray; it produces intimacy with the One *to* whom you pray; it produces intimacy with the one *with* whom you pray." I could not possibly agree more. Our first feeble attempts at sharing and transparency may have seemed awkward to some, like watching a baby learn to stand up and then take its first few, humbling steps. But the incubator of prayer nurtured our young desire for love and understanding between one another, and we determined to press on in The Climb.

Three years ago—the week immediately following our first prayer summit—the pastors of this community agreed to set aside one hour on Wednesdays at noon. Our commitment takes us all the way to the third floor, the Family Life Pavilion of the First Baptist Church here in Modesto. Sometimes we walk up the steps. Sometimes we ride the elevator. But always, we climb. Higher than at any other moment in our week. Our only agenda as we gather: intercede for our community and one another.

There are Lutherans, Baptists, Pentecostals, Independents, and Nazarenes. Black men, White men, Hispanics, and Asians pray together. All standing for Jesus. All kneeling before God. That's how we climb together. We climb by kneeling.

We have seen some incredible things transpire here in Modesto since our weekly concert of prayer began. One year after we began our noon meetings, one of our local churches sponsored a musical presentation, "Heaven's Gates and Hell's Flames."

Nearly eighty thousand people—yes, eighty thousand—attended during the musical's run of several weeks. Most important, thousands of people made first-time decisions for Christ. And during that time, the pastors in this community gathered every Wednesday to intercede and thank God for what he was doing in another pastor's church. And the pastor of the church hosting the musical gladly sent many names of those receiving Christ in his church to other churches and pastors in town for follow-up. Remarkable.

I love the men of God I pray with every week. And I know they love me. When we gather, before we pray, we greet each other. We embrace. Holy hugs and kisses for brothers we haven't seen in seven whole days. Genuine love and care wells within each one of us every time we meet.

That is not to say that we have arrived, that we have attained a totally mature sense of spiritual well-being. Every pastor in our community would tell you that some undesirable divisions and distinctives still mark our congregations, our lives, and our ministries. Sometimes they are petty. Sometimes they revolve around theological or ecclesiastical differences. Sometimes, God forbid, they are nothing more than titanic egos clashing with one another. No, we have not arrived. But then, "evangelical nirvana" has never been our goal. We strive for commitment—to one another, and to The Climb.

We have determined to pray in the midst of it all.

Pray in spite of it all.

Acknowledge, once and for all . . . that none of us is king of the mountain.

One cold winter day, a woman walked through vacant, empty streets. She did not seem to mind that the shops of Sychar were closed now, that the merchants had already retired to the warmth of their homes and crackling fires. According to Roman time, it was about six in the evening. Her destination: Jacob's well. She went there every day to draw from its deep pool. A certain monotony possessed her; a plainness and sameness gathered around her as she walked. Her life droned on from one sorry day to the next. Empty days. Empty as the clay pot she carried in her cold hands.

Each evening about this time, she made her way to that well. A daily chore to fill a clay pot, then a heavy walk home with the weight of another day's supply of water on her head, and the weight of the world on her shoulders.

What thoughts coursed through her mind as she walked? She may have been lonely. The gloom of winter's dusk may have clouded her thoughts. Or perhaps she was bitter that the cold rejection of other women in Sychar forced her to draw water at this late hour, rather than at midday when the sun could warm her. We cannot say with assurance. We only know she walked through those city streets alone. She would draw from the well in silence, and then return to her home.

As she neared Jacob's well, she noticed a man. She didn't recognize him; the visitor sat alone, and looked as if he were waiting for someone. She did not speak. She knew. Without a word passing between them, she could feel him watching her. And she already knew this man despised her. He wore familiar dress—clearly Jewish, and all Jews hated the racially mixed Samaritans. Although their eyes did not meet, she knew the contempt that invariably glared from the eyes of Jewish men. She had probably seen it many times before.

Who would have imagined? A solitary Jewish man. A lonely Samaritan woman. A walk to Jacob's well. A picture of divine appointment. She was about to receive an invitation to The Climb.

Now the stranger spoke. A remarkable request. And she wondered, *Why would this blue-blood Jewish man be asking for water from a half-breed Samaritan woman?*

"Will you give me a drink?" he asked. A simple question for some, perhaps. But very complex for her.

When she heard the question, she turned to look into his face. It was almost as if she could not believe her ears. That he would even speak was remarkable. But to ask her for something to drink seemed incredible. She felt a need to clarify.

"You are a Jew; I am a Samaritan. We don't associate, do we?" Very improper. Very improbable.

He spoke again. "If you only knew . . ." he said.

But she did not know—how could she know—the identity of this stranger. His conversation spread in ever-widening concentric circles, farther and farther from reality. Was he asking her for a drink . . . or offering her a drink? Which was it? Gift of God? Which God? Whose God? And the living water of which he spoke? Where was this well? Very confusing for a tired woman at the end of a long day. Probably a very awkward moment for her.

"Sir," she said, "you have nothing to draw with and the well is deep." She decided to break the tension by saying the obvious. *He isn't suggesting that I use my pot to give him a drink—or is he? Maybe he is at the wrong well. This well belongs to Jacob. Which well is he looking for?*

She was not aware of any "living water" well, but the well where they stood was significant. Deep. A gift. *Yes, maybe that's what he means. Jacob gave us this well. He's talking about an inheritance.*

For the third time, now, the stranger spoke. "Everyone who drinks this water will be thirsty again, but whoever drinks the water I give him will never thirst. Indeed, the water I give him will become in him a spring of water welling up to eternal life."

What is this continual mention of "living water"? And the spring he speaks of, which flows from the inside out? The wearied woman listened; though confused, her lean soul seemed to take sustenance and hope from the promise of this unusual man. Oh, how she wished for a well like the one he described. Tired of the walk. Weary and wearied from the cold of winter. The perfect solution: a "one-drink-and-you-will-be-forever-and-eternally" well. Like salt on bread, the man's words created a thirst to be satisfied. And so she asked *him* for a drink.

"Sir, give me this water so that I won't get thirsty and have to keep coming back to draw water."

The conversation quickened. "Go get your husband and come back," said the man. And the woman of Samaria unwittingly exposed the naked truth about her life.

"I have no husband."

"Quite true," said the stranger, declaring that she had been married five times. Five attempts at marital bliss. Five dismal failures . . . and still counting. The sixth man had not bothered to solemnize their intimacy with a marriage contract. She lived on a street called adultery.

Quick now. Change the subject, she thought. *Since the man is obviously a prophet, divert his thoughts toward God and worship, and he will forget about marital status.*

"Sir, . . . our fathers worshiped on this mountain, but you Jews claim that the place where we must worship is in Jerusalem." She had expressed a deeper searching. *Where should we worship God? On this mountain or some other? Which mountain has the truth at the top?* And she turned the conversation toward The Climb.

I will not tell you the rest of this story. You can read it for yourself in John 4. I will only tell you this. When Jesus answered the woman's question about where to worship God, he did not give directions to the nearest Baptist church. He did not explain the superior ways of the Lutherans, nor describe the exhilaration of the Pentecostals. He failed to mention Calvinism; he didn't bring up Arminianism either. In fact, he didn't even point to the third floor of a specific building where godly men had gathered.

The stranger didn't specify the obvious advantages of being an independent church. He offered no dunking or sprinkling or immersing instructions. For some reason, the Master neglected to leave directions on whether she and her Samaritan neighbors should sing songs from the hymnal or choruses drawn from Old Testament Scriptures. He gave no specifics of ritual: Should we stand to sing the third verse, or should we sing the third verse . . . and then stand? Do we raise our hands? Do we speak in tongues? Should we associate with people who do . . . or don't? Should we have a choir? Or a worship team? Or both? Or neither? He didn't say.

That may seem curious. Why couldn't he see how desperately we need to know the answers to these and other important questions if we're going to have church the way we're supposed to? Not one word about style, or differences, or labels we paste on the signs in front of our churches. Nothing about theology, or ritual, or custom. And what about being "user-friendly"—is that okay? It would have simplified things so much if he had just said a word about the appropriateness of a "seeker's service."

Well, he did. Check it out for yourself in verses 23–24.

He told the woman at the well one very important truth: Worship must be directed toward and sensitive to the Seeker—the One who searches the hearts and lives of men and women. And worship that is not in spirit and truth is not Seeker-sensitive. The success of our efforts and the quality of our worship depend not on the diversity of our labels or the location of our denominational headquarters. Worship flows from the intent and determined unity of our hearts. The richness of our traditions, as wonderful as many of them are, will never satiate or satisfy the hunger and thirst of the lost.

He knew how to quench thirst on that cold day in the winter of her life. And he offered the way toward wellness at the well. The Living Water knew that to climb to God one does not climb a specific mountain; one kneels before God and drinks of lasting water in a relationship with him. The way to God is not how-to's nor the name of a mountain, nor a denomination either. He declared, "God is spirit, and those who worship Him must worship in spirit and truth" (John 4:24 NASB).

If your deepest desire is to worship him, lock hearts and lives with those around you who are of like precious faith, regardless of their background, label, or tongue. If you're feeling a need for a different mountain on which to worship, don't be so sure you need to go find a new church. Maybe you just need a new perspective. Maybe you need to climb more often to that third floor, which is prayer. Gather with a few friends and climb the mountain of prayer for the lost. If you need a formula for what to say when you get together, this one will do as well as any when you're praying for the lost: "God have mercy on them all . . . God have mercy on us all."

10

What's a Mother to Do?

Occasionally, events demand my attendance on Saturday evenings: weddings, receptions, fiftieth wedding anniversaries. But these occasions are the exceptions, not the rule. On most Saturdays, I begin early in the day to think about Sunday and what it holds—about my message and what I have prepared to share with the people of God. I just don't "do" Saturday nights.

A little over a year ago, however, on the Saturday night before Mother's Day, my wife and I chose to attend a special dinner sponsored by a Chinese church that meets in our church facility. It was a loud, freewheeling affair with wonderful Chinese food and an atmosphere typical of these warmly animated people. We didn't stay long, though. In fact, we left about seven-thirty. I wanted to get home before too late.

On the way home, I noticed flashing red lights and emergency equipment just a few blocks from our house. As we neared the scene of what was obviously an accident, we saw the two cars that had been involved. One of the cars was small and teal and foreign. The front end of the car looked as if a giant hand had crushed it like an empty pop can. Rust-colored water pooled beneath its ruptured radiator; green antifreeze covered the pavement; shattered red and yellow plastic sprinkled the roadway, creating an eerie, jagged stained-glass picture. There were no passengers in the car.

People stood watching, looking, pointing at the wreckage, and shaking their heads. We slowed as we drove by the scene. I hoped to myself that this was not one of my neighbors.

Then I noticed the other car. It, too, was a small car, crumpled and mangled and exposed in places not meant to be seen from the outside. But it was not a foreign car—not to me, anyway. This car was Nathan's car—Nathan, our second son, Nathan, our twenty-year-old. It belonged to our Nathan, who is kind, gentle, and not at all like the violence of this accident scene. I knew it was Nathan's car because of the small, rusty dent in the rear bumper. I knew this bumper. I knew this car. I knew this driver, this grown child—this son of ours whose name means *Gift of God.*

As we pulled to the side of this scene, Randee and I looked with quick and searching eyes. We looked for his tall, broad frame. Where was that blond head of his in the crowd of onlookers? *He must be here somewhere,* I said to myself as we approached the sickening sight of the car. The windshield bulged with an ominous break from the inside, near the steering wheel. I prayed silently that it hadn't been smashed by someone's face. The door on the driver's side gaped open, torn by "Jaws of Life" and hands of mercy that ripped it off its hinges.

Police were on the scene, too. One of them directed traffic, motioning for people he supposed were gawkers (like my wife and me) to keep moving. Another officer bent over the hood of one of the cars, working on an accident report.

As we approached, I found myself desperately needing answers to questions I didn't want to ask. *Am I right? Is this mangled wreck my son's car? Was he driving? Was he hurt? Where? How?*

"I think my son may have been driving this car," I said almost apologetically to the officer. He looked up from his writing and noticed us, noticed our parental presence. My wife stood at my side, her hands cupping her mouth as if to hush her anxiety, as if she were trying to hold back words that wanted out.

"Big guy?" the officer asked as he made a measured gesture with his arms, perfectly describing my son's broad shoulders.

"Yes," I said. "Yes, he's a big kid."

"Blond?" asked the officer. Again, I confirmed with a nod of my head. But now, my wife could not contain her words. Her hands moved from the front of her mouth to the sides of her face, as if cradling it. Her eyes dropped to the report the officer was writing and the driver's license pinched under the top of his clipboard. She spoke with a certain urgency as she asked the question.

"Nathan?" she asked. "Was his name Nathan?" As the answer from the officer came back with a nod, her hands again took their place across her mouth, as fear and anxiety touched her face. Her eyes followed the officer's glance down toward the report he wrote and the license beneath his clipboard.

"That's him. Nathan Jones," said the officer.

"Is he hurt? Where is he?" asked his mother.

Now, the answers to the questions seemed to take forever to form in the mouth of the policeman. He talked too slowly for parents hanging on the edge of his every word.

"He just left in the ambulance. A bump on his head, a broken arm, maybe a few broken ribs. Didn't look to be too serious." *Serious* may have more than one definition when you stand alongside a windshield that's been smashed from the inside out, broken by the face of your second son. *Urgent*. Our Nathan's condition may not have been serious to the policeman, but our need to see him felt urgent. As the policeman's words trailed off into the wind, Randee had already wheeled on her heels, and her mother-hands reached toward our car door, as we hurried away from this scene.

We drove to the hospital. Controlled and quiet we were. No need for panic; no need to let our minds race down roads cluttered with things we could not know. When we arrived, we found Nathan lying on an emergency room gurney just outside one of the examining rooms. Nurses had propped his arm on two pillows. A grotesque bend slightly above his left wrist made me know the officer's assessment was correct: Nathan did indeed have a broken arm. A pleasant nurse walked up to us as we stood next to Nathan and said they would keep him overnight because the arm would need surgery. The doctor had said that otherwise he was fine.

But before Randee believed he was fine, she needed a second opinion—her own. Impervious to the staff, she did her own quick, "I'm-the-mother-so-don't-even-think-of-asking-me-to-leave" sort of examination of Nathan's injuries. All the while, the hospital personnel (who acted immune to this unsolicited parental virus) casually worked and talked and laughed as our son lay in agony in the emergency room.

It was good to hear my son's voice. It was good to see his face, unmarred except for a bump on his forehead. (He made out a lot better than the windshield!) After I'd had a chance to check out Nathan's condition for myself, I knew I needed to make a call.

Low, and bent near Nathan's ear so he could hear, I made a call to the Great Physician to ask for his healing touch. I know people watched me as I leaned over my boy to pray in the hall, but I didn't care. My dry, nervous throat was lumped with emotion as I thanked God that he protected my boy from a Saturday night disaster.

If you're like me, you pray every time something happens to one of your kids. When our kids come into the world, we know that they will suffer many bumps and bruises along the path of life. Some of the injuries will be physical, some will be emotional, some social or spiritual. So when my kids go through something tough, I pray.

The Climb toward maturity often leads to perilous parental moments, unexpected, unwanted, and unknown.

But he who never sleeps nor slumbers remains on duty. We can trust him to give his acute care to every detail and moment. And nothing escapes his compassionate touch.

She experienced that—the woman, I mean. The one in the sad parade. The one who cried. You may know her story already, but I will tell you again.

One day a parade took place about five miles southeast of Nazareth. A slow parade made its way through the streets of a town called Nain, which means *pleasant, delightful*. But this was not a pleasant day. And this was not a delightful parade. A large crowd of people marched in slow and deliberate cadence. The men in front of the crowd carried the body of a young man, who lay on a funeral bier, or coffin. A woman dressed in black mourning clothes followed closely behind the body of the young man. He was her son, her only son, and she was a widow.

She wept and mourned as she walked, probably having had little time to deal with the tragedy of her son's death. The custom of Eastern cultures demanded that the same day a person died, the body would be buried. And so in one day, the widowed woman would go from enjoying the solace and comfort of an only son to watching him die, burying him, and then returning home to live the rest of her life in the despair and aloneness of it all. Sorrow sucked the very breath from her soul as she walked along behind the dead boy—the boy who had been her life.

As the funeral procession came to the town gate, another crowd of people approached from the opposite direction. An only Son led this crowd, too, but he was not dead. He was very much alive, and the crowd that followed him hung on his every word. Many of them did not understand his true identity, but they followed him because of the incredible miracles he performed and the wisdom of his teaching.

As Jesus approached the gate, The Climb now took him into the midst of the processional coming toward him. His heart went out to that weeping woman. If anyone knew what it would be like to lose an only son, he knew.

As he walked toward the crowd of people, perhaps his all-seeing eyes caught a flash or glimpse of a day yet to come, when another mother—his own—would weep for her Son. Perhaps he felt a tinge of the sting of death and decided to play the part of a grave-robber. We do not know what he felt, exactly. We only know that the sight and sound of a sobbing mother moved him deeply, and with a quiet authority he determined to interrupt her grief. He stopped the proceedings. He brought comfort to a mother's heart.

He said, "Don't cry."

He touched her with his words, but he wasn't finished yet. Then he touched the coffin. He reached out with his very hand and touched the coffin of the mother's only son. Those carrying the boy's body stopped in their tracks. It was time for him to say a few appropriate words over the body of the recently departed. It was time he brought death to a grinding halt.

"Young man," he said, "I say to you, get up!"

And he did. The young man did sit up. He talked. He moved. He acted in a totally inappropriate way for someone about to be buried. The corpse isn't supposed to hop down and walk home right in the middle of the service. Imagine it. One minute, he was the guest of honor at a solemn gathering. The next, he was a boy acting like a kid again. It was obvious he'd never been to his own funeral before.

And Jesus gave him back to his mother, a gift of God a second time.

Even after this incredible miracle, some people still struggled with Jesus' identity. Doctor Luke tells us in the seventh chapter of his Gospel that shortly after this event, even John the Baptist had questions about who Jesus was. But I'll bet this mother didn't have any questions. Not this widowed woman who walked behind a dead body until she met the Great Physician. Some might call him Teacher. Some might call him Messiah. There are many names that depict his glory and identify who he is. But if you could ask her, I believe she would call him the Son. She would tell you, "No doubt in my mind. He's God's Son, all right. It had to be *God's* Son . . . who spoke to *my* son that day."

11 White Space

A Japanese artist was commissioned by an American to do a painting. The completed work had, in a lower corner, the branch of a cherry tree with a few blossoms and a bird perched upon it. The entire upper half of the painting was white. Unhappily, the American asked the artist to put something else in the painting, because it looked so, well, bare. The Japanese artist refused the request. When pressed for an explanation, the artist said if he did fill up the painting, there would be no space for the bird . . . to fly.

Robert A. Rosenstone, *Mirror in the Stone*[1]

A few months ago, I was scheduled to speak at a retreat for men in Washington State. On that same weekend, Randee had been invited to take a trip out of state with one of her friends. We don't go our separate ways very often, but for three days on our calendar that's what we had planned.

About ten days before the men's retreat, however, I received a call saying the weekend had been postponed. The coordinator said they would try to reschedule later in the year. I couldn't believe it. My calendar had a hole—three days with no appointments, no counseling, no staff meetings, no preaching on Sunday. Nothing.

Since Randee's trip with her friend had been planned for several weeks, and her airfare and accommodations were already worked out, I told her to go and enjoy her time with her friend. I'd make do.

And so on one sunny Thursday afternoon, I told my secretary I'd be out for the next three days and not available on my cellular phone unless it was an emergency. Then I went home and packed a small bag of necessities, tossed them in the trunk of the car, and started to drive. For some reason, I felt like a teenage kid out with the family car for the first time after he got his driver's license. I had no destination in particular. Just a road. No map. Three days, and no agenda. What a gift, really.

I drove to our local Christian bookstore and bought three books I had been wanting to read. Then I walked outside and spit in the wind. It blew toward San Francisco, and I took that as God's leading for my life at that moment. I drove out of the parking lot and headed almost due west toward what we locals in northern California call "The City."

As I drove, I began to develop a plan for the next three days. I'd find some inexpensive little motel and hole up to read and write and pray. I'd walk on the beach if I wanted. I'd sit and watch people in shopping malls if I wanted. Three days to do nothing . . . but what I wanted.

I enjoyed a rare and spontaneous anonymity while I was away, a planned amnesia of identity. I was all alone. A wedding ring on my finger, but no wife at my side. Still a pastor, but incognito. A dad, sans sons. I recognized no one. And no one knew me. Not one question from anyone. No one even spoke to me in all that time, except one guy who acted like he was in a real hurry. (He stopped me on a street corner and asked, "Have you got the time?" Of course, I knew what he wanted, and I did "give him the time." But later I sat down and thought about what a strange question that is when you get right down to it. We ask people if they've "got the time" the same way we'd ask them if they've "got the measles." Was he trying to "catch" the time? Did the guy who asked me the question want to "borrow" some time? I found it interesting that he asked me if I "had the time." Did I "have the time" for what?)

I planned no itinerary nor did I keep a schedule of events. I had no set time to eat, sleep, or be any particular place at all. I didn't sleep in, because sleeping late doesn't recharge my battery. (In fact, there are times when I feel as though sleeping is a waste of time.) I didn't eat much, either, because I wasn't that hungry. But when I ate, I ate what I wanted.

One morning, I decided to explore the shops in Jack London Square in Oakland. In one of them, a great bookstore, I picked up a neat book on solitude and being alone. Then I walked about two blocks to the ferry stop. I bought a ticket and took a ferry ride around the bay and San Francisco, all by myself; rode right under the Bay Bridge and looked up at it from the underside. That same morning, I caught a cable car into the inner recesses of "The City." I sat and read books in oak-paneled coffee haunts, unusual places that felt engaging and quaint. I took on the persona of some Bohemian free spirit, out to see the world without the world looking back or even noticing I was there. After an hour or so in one spot, I would change venues—another coffeehouse, another quiet place to read and write and think.

I could feel it: My batteries were recharging. My inner man was being renewed. Over the course of three days and nights of anonymity and solitude, a fresh view of my world and my God restored my soul.

I recently read a great quote by Thomas Szasz in *The Second Sin:* "Man cannot long survive without air, water, and sleep. Next in importance comes food. And close on its heels, solitude."[2] Ever since I took my three-day jaunt all alone, I think he's right.

Jesus understood solitude, too. He didn't clamber over the rocks and rills of life twenty-four hours a day. He occasionally secluded himself to pray and be alone, away from the demands of others. In the midst of making bread, calming storms, and soothing pain, he "found" the time or "took" the time or "spent" the time necessary to accommodate a rare, solitaire gem: aloneness. Of course it didn't come easy. Expensive. So many "needed" him. So many all around him. In order to achieve the aloneness his soul required, the consummate servant had to take his leave of the din of it all, and give himself the permission to climb toward a mountain of retreat.

He climbed the Mount of Olives and other hillsides near his points of ministry and spent time with the Father restoring his soul. The line of his life drew a sparse and silent picture: a mountain called seclusion. On a canvas intentionally painted in the storm and winter of The Climb, he unapologetically created a white space of nothing to allow room for flight to the Father.

In my time of aloneness, I had many opportunities to reflect upon how good it can be to be alone. I distilled my thinking into a short list of three observations, three fleeting thoughts about The Climb and seclusion.

First, we must occasionally experience solitude. Realize it. Commit to it. Next to God and air and water and food and sleep—we need solitude. Stop. Plan. For your sake. For God's sake.

Give yourself permission to spit in the wind and see if the Spirit will not blow you to some place of seclusion with him. The Climb demands it. The climb will be worth it.

Second, if you visit the mountain called seclusion, you may decide the view is so refreshing you don't want to go back to the noise and clamor of life. You don't want to go home. Suppress that urge, should it visit your thinking. Solitude is a fabulous place to visit, but believe me, you don't want to live there. (Ask any monk.)

Third, and perhaps most importantly: Be careful what you do when you are all alone and no one but God knows where you are. Though time alone can be a great opportunity to hear from him, it also can become a prime occasion when the enemy can come and tempt us in ways we would not be vulnerable to if we were with others committed to The Climb. A fallen climber on the mountainside is still fallen . . . even if God is the only one there to know, so guard yourself when you are alone.

12

A Novel Idea

Writing a book about commitment in The Climb of faith presents some tough challenges for a writer. A couple of reasons make that so. First, anytime a person writes a book about anything, the reader has a reasonable responsibility to question the credentials of the person writing the book. I mean, does he or she have a "right to write"? If the book deals with children and discipline, the reader may ask, legitimately, I believe, "How did his kids turn out?" If a husband and wife writing team is teaching on marriage and family, the reader may wonder, *How many years have they been married themselves, and how do I know that they're practicing their own preaching?* And if someone is writing on commitment, well then, how committed is he? And to what or whom?

The second reason a book on commitment is difficult to write is a little more complex. Since you're holding this book in your hands reading it, you have probably been to a bookstore recently and know the vast amount of wonderful material available to encourage devotion and commitment to Christ. Will one more book help? Will one more book produce change? If the availability of materials on the topic of commitment actually produced commitment in the lives of people, we in the church in America would be the most committed people on the face of the earth.

But we are not. We still struggle in even the simple things.

Did you know that experts on church growth say that the average Sunday attendance across America would increase by 50 percent if the people who normally come once a month would come twice a month, and the people who come twice a month would come three times a month? A 50 percent growth by just having people commit to show up to church! Just imagine. If someone could discover the formula that would get all the people in Christ's body to commit to just one more Sunday a month, the church would grow incredibly overnight.

Since you've made it this far through this book, you know that commitment is the major issue of The Climb; clearly I haven't yet been able to unbottle the secret to church growth and commitment. And in my call to greater devotion, I've tried to stay away from pat formulas and didactic approaches. (I did have "three fleeting thoughts" at the end of the previous chapter, but cut me some slack, will you?) I've left out stuff like "the five reasons you've gotta do it this way," and "the seven most important elements of a spiritual existence." I know we've come this far in the book and I still haven't mentioned "the three things you should never forget."

There's a very good reason I refrained from doing so. You want to know why? Okay, I'll tell you.

But first, I will tell you three short stories . . . and then I will answer that question. Are they true stories? We know two of them are, for they are recorded in the Holy Writ. The one in the middle? I will let you decide.

The Rebuke

For several days, Jesus had been teaching in the area of Caesarea Philippi, asking his disciples if they really understood who he was, and preparing them for what would surely come. He explained to them in clear and certain words that he must die and then be raised on the third day.

Peter, however, choked on that morbid truth and drew the Lord aside to try to dissuade him.

"Never, Lord. This will never happen to you!" chided Peter.

A stern rebuke from this "friend" of God. Peter would not permit this awful thing. He knew—everyone knows—that kings crush resistance. They don't tolerate it; they don't submit to it. They certainly don't die because of it. And so Peter's words—God-forsaking words, God-betraying words.

"Never, Lord," said the bold and brave fisherman.

Perhaps a foreshadowing that Peter would cut the ear off any man who tried to lay a hand on his Lord. To Jesus, the words hinted at vaporous commitment, loyalty that would disappear with the smoke of denial's fire. The words came from one who did not know the meaning of an empty tomb.

But Peter's sharp words were drawn from a scabbard of human design and not the will of the Father. Jesus would not be wounded by the words of this ignorant and uninformed man. "Behind me, Satan," said the Master.

Committed to The Climb, Jesus set his face toward the "It is finished!" line. And he would not be turned aside. Instead, the Master brought a sober invitation for all who would hear: "Deny yourself, take up your cross and follow me."

The Invitation

Late one summer, just before the harvesttime, a courier made his way through the courts of heaven. "Where is he going in such a hurry, holy Lord?" asked the angelic hosts. But the God of heaven did not speak. He knew the answer would be revealed to them soon enough. The messenger carried an urgency about him; his manner and his walk betrayed a certain presage, a portent of things to come.

The angels marked his way, and they noticed that he moved toward two familiar faces in their midst. Two men, once mortals but now residents of heaven, Moses and Elijah, who sat in the hallowed awe and presence of God. The messenger approached the two and handed them a scroll of lambskin, white and beautiful.

As the two ancient ones reached for the scroll, the angels could see the royal seal of the Prince himself emblazoned on the lambskin. The men touched the seal with great reverence, almost as if they hesitated to move beyond the wonder of the Name depicted on the seal. But finally, they opened their royal correspondence and began to read. They held the message in their hands for many moments, as if they were reading the contents over and over, as if they could not believe their eyes.

"What does it say?" asked one of the angels. Others among the heavenly host wondered. *Is it a let-*

ter? Is it a song? A poem perhaps, or a list of names? The heavenly host wondered to themselves what the message disclosed, though they held their peace, waiting for the two men to respond.

But Moses and Elijah said nothing. And they did not read aloud. Instead, they stood, faced the heavenly Father, and prostrated themselves before the throne of God for many moments in absolute silence. Finally, with all of heaven watching, they stood and walked away. As they left the throne, they handed the lambskin to one of the angelic hosts.

He read it and realized what it was. An invitation. A divine summons. The Prince had issued an invitation to attend and wrote it in his own hand. It read:

The Prince of heaven requests your presence.
Time: Soon
Location: A consecrated place
The Occasion: A conversation with the King
Dress: Formal white

Then he read the contents aloud to all who had gathered. And the angels began a holy chorus, while obedient footsteps of the two friends of God echoed down the corridors.

The Sanctuary

Jesus chose three disciples, Peter, James, and John, to walk with him high up on a mountain, probably Mount Hermon (which means a *consecrated place*, a *sanctuary*). There the four began to pray. Three of them were very sleepy and dozed; the Lord was wide awake. And as he prayed, his countenance and visage changed. Transfigured. His robe became white, white as bleached cotton. The humble servant dressed in flashy clothes—clothes bright as a bolt of lightning.

The three bleary-eyed companions stirred from their sleepiness and saw the wonder of it all. And as if the sight of the Master in such glory was not enough to frighten them witless, they noticed another incredible thing. For the four on the mountain were now six. Elijah and Moses appeared, and they stood next to Jesus there on that holy incline. They, too, were clothed in brilliance and glory. They talked with their sovereign about the fulfillment of his departure soon to take place in Jerusalem.

It was probably not a long conversation, but long enough for the three frightened disciples. As Moses and Elijah left the presence of the Lord, Peter spoke again. Always the mouth. Always the first to speak up, even if it was wrong . . . even if he had no idea what to say.

"It's good for us to be here. Let's build three houses—one for you, one for Elijah, one for Moses." Perhaps impudent Peter babbled without thinking in his effort to honor the three holy men before him. But what—on earth—would those three need with a house? When you've been at home in glory, everything else pales by comparison.

Then, a cloud. And a voice.

And God, who said, "This is my Son, whom I love. Listen to him!" The three companions of Jesus fell on their faces, petrified and nearly dead as tombstones, for it is an awesome thing to hear God speak. But Jesus came and touched their frightened lives and said, "Get up," and, "Don't be afraid." He told them not to say a word to anyone about the events they had seen.

And they did not.

They kept the matters to themselves, although they did discuss with each other what "rising from the dead" meant.

Ready for my answer as to why I didn't include any "Top Ten Reasons" or "The Five Biggest Obstacles" in this book? Okay, I'll tell you. It's too easy to skip over pat answers, and the writer in me wants to leave out all the stuff readers usually skip. That's why I tell stories, that's why I leave out lists.

But perhaps you're one of those who loves outlines and structures to help you remember things. In that case, here's the best I can do. You have just read three stories of people who have a lot in common with you and me. It may not seem so on the surface, but check it out again. A trilogy of characters trying to get a grip in the midst of The Climb.

One man rebuked. Peter learned never say "never" to Jesus if you plan to climb with him. Oh, and by the way, or along the way, or in the way, all you have to do to be committed to The Climb is deny yourself, pick up your cross, and follow him. Simple as a list of one, two, three, right?

Two men invited. A pretend story that didn't really happen . . . or did it? After all, we do know Elijah and Moses made a fleeting guest appearance on the mount. But did they actually get an invitation and have to decide whether to come? Has there ever been a time when old ones in the faith were ready when called, humbled to be invited, and in his presence when the invitation to deeper fellowship showed up?

I think so. Such invitations do come, and I take great encouragement in watching the old saints still among us who faithfully continue to accept the call. Keep your eyes on the old ones with gray hair; they know The Climb, they still talk with God, and he talks with them.

Three men afraid, sleeping in the sanctuary again. Peter, James, and John almost missed the message, frightened nearly to death at the fact that God actually showed up. They would never forget that the road to transformation and commitment always goes over the top of a mountain called consecration. They struggled at the thought, at the bad news that was good. Such a novel idea, a remarkable detail they could not skip over: *The only way to commit to The*

Climb is to die to self. They walked away mumbling, struggling with commitment and confused about exactly what he had in mind.

Perhaps they were like a child, the child who wrote the letter to God: "Dear God, What's it like to die? I don't wanna do it; I just wanna know what it's like."

If God chose to answer that letter, I believe this is what he would say: "Follow me, and you will find out."

13

Cheers for the Family

I will tell you a story I've never told another living soul—not my wife, nor my parents, nor my brothers, nor my sister. I had forgotten all about it until last fall, when it came back to me. No one in the whole world knows this story but me . . . unless you, too, by some strange coincidence, may have happened on it, once upon a time.

Eminence is a common little town, really—the county seat of Shannon County, Missouri, about two hundred miles southwest of St. Louis. The word *eminence* has two common definitions: (1) a high and lofty place or thing, such as a hill; and (2) superiority in rank, position, character, achievement;

greatness; celebrity. But a visit to this town would offer no sense of an elevated or superior place. Visit Eminence someday, and you will feel you are back in early rural America.

Drive south along the main street in town. You'll pass the county courthouse on your right. On the front lawn of that old and stately courthouse, you'll spy a rustic log cabin, which has been reassembled by the county residents. I say reassembled because the old cabin was discovered in a remote area of the county called Possum Trot a few years ago, and the local folks carefully and lovingly disassembled it, and then reassembled it on the lawn of the county courthouse. The tiny old house is more than 115 years old and an important part of the history of Shannon County.

That cabin that sits on the courthouse lawn represents an important part of my history, too. My great-great-grandfather cut and split the logs he needed, and then built that very cabin himself. In fact, my great-grandmother, my maternal and paternal grandparents, and both my parents were raised in Eminence.

What I mean to say is that if you were to carefully examine every branch and leaf and limb of my family tree, when you finally came to the roots, you would find Eminence. I never lived there, but I consider myself "country" in my bones. I spent many weekends visiting my grandparents and other family members and friends during my growing-up years. Eminence was (and still is) a very important place to me.

And, Eminence had a town baseball team.

As I mentioned earlier, my hometown is Granite City, Illinois. I grew up in a neighborhood that had a lot of kids, and we survived the long, hot summers by choosing up teams nearly every day and playing baseball. I loved to play baseball. I played almost every day of the summer. Most mornings, I would get up early, and my brother Dan and I would take off with a bunch of other kids to a place we called Green Field, a glorified sandlot with grass, but also a place with real character.

It was probably only two acres or so, though it seemed such an expansive place to me while growing up. On one end of that two-acre parcel, well-worn base paths marked the outline of our ball field. Water from overnight thunderstorms used to puddle up along the base paths and around home plate. Sliding into home represented a unique joy, especially for those kids with the nerve to try it head first. We all knew where the tricky spots on the field were, too. For example, a ball hit down the line in right field had a great chance to be stretched into a double; the slight dip in the ground in right field (actually it was a hole) caused more than one kid to fall flat on his face trying to field the ball.

Every kid in our neighborhood knew every bump and blemish in Green Field because we virtually lived there every day of the summer. We'd play there sometimes until nearly dark. I was one of the oldest kids in our neighborhood, so invariably I picked myself as one of the team captains. It usually worked.

I would describe my game as "adequate." Not great. Not really that bad. Just in the middle somewhere. Perhaps an occasional moment of brilliance, interspersed with long periods of mediocrity. But because of my love for the game, and the fact that I grew up in the heartland of St. Louis Cardinals country, I spent many hours pretending I was a great ballplayer, imagining myself to be Stan Musial or the great Bob Gibson.

One day, my dad came home from work and said some guys in Granite City had approached him about helping to put a team of young ballplayers together to make a trip to Eminence; the Granite City team would play ball against the town team. If I wanted to go, I could.

A chance to make a trip nearly two hundred miles just to play ball! I knew a lot of people in Eminence. I had many relatives in that town. And now, I was going to go with some friends from my hometown to play the team from Eminence. It sounded great.

We left Granite City about five-thirty one Friday afternoon and drove four hours to get to Eminence.

When we pulled into town, I felt a strange sensation—like a man without a country, perhaps, or a man with two countries, and I was about to choose which one I liked best. Our caravan of three or four station wagons drove straight to the ballpark just to get a look at where we would be playing on Saturday and Sunday.

I, of course, had been there many times. But most of the guys on our team of twelve- to fourteen-year-olds had never been to Eminence. They had never seen the town ball field. It had lights. It had a fence all the way around the outfield. It had bleachers so people could come and sit and watch the game, and bench seats that began behind home plate and wrapped like a fan down the first and third baselines.

No doubt about it. This was no Green Field. This was no sandlot. This was big-league, a significant place to play ball.

We played three games—one Saturday night under the lights, and a Sunday doubleheader after church. I say "we" played three games, but that's not exactly the truth. Personally I didn't play at all on Saturday night. All my relatives came to see me play, but I didn't get in. I sat on the bench. I don't think the coach knew. He didn't act like he knew or understood how important this was to me. My roots were here. My family and friends were here to see me.

I tried to be as conspicuous as possible on the bench. I tried to look as much like a baseball player as I could. I made a lot of noise. I spat on the ground and occasionally rubbed dirt on my hands, making sure some of it got on my uniform so I would look as hot and dirty and "in the game" as the guys who were actually playing. I wanted it to seem as if I was an integral part of the team and that they were saving me for a time when they really needed me. Well, they didn't really need me on Saturday night. Close game, though. We lost, six to four.

They didn't need me in Sunday's first game either. Again, all my relatives and friends showed up. I felt their eyes searching the horizon of the outfield, specifically left field, where I should have been.

But they looked too high. *Lower. Lower, to the bench. Follow the noise. The one rubbing the dirt in his hands. The one who spits and sweats. How did he get his uniform so dirty sitting on the bench?*

We lost the first game of the Sunday doubleheader; I don't remember the score, but the word *slaughtered* would probably not be too strong a word to use. They cleaned our clocks. Between the first and second game of the doubleheader, the coach took us all out into center field. The guys who had played Saturday night and had just finished nine innings looked exhausted. They sipped water and turned their hats backwards and flopped down on the outfield grass, disgusted at such a poor showing.

The coach gave an inspiring challenge before the second game. He used baseball language; phrases like "hunker down" and "execute the fundamentals" seemed to pepper his pep talk. "Outfielders, you gotta remember to hit the cutoff man," he said. "When you're at the plate, watch the third-base coach for the hitting signs," he said. "Be aggressive with your bats," he said. And we all listened.

But I think some of us listened more intently than others.

My chance to play on Sunday afternoon came late in the day, about the fifth or sixth inning.

"Jones, take left field," said the coach. And so I did. I raced as fast as I could to my position. Most of my relatives had gone home by that time. But both my grandpas were still there to watch. I did a decent job in the outfield, fielding several balls hit my way. I even threw out a runner trying to stretch a single into a double. But the thing I remember more than anything else was my trip to the plate in the ninth inning.

I don't remember the score, only that it would take a couple of five-run homers to put us in the game. I don't remember if there were runners on. I only remember that several of the townspeople were watching me hit, and I felt like the city boy from Granite City. Not one of theirs, really. But they were polite. Frankie Bob Finch or some such guy was pitching. I don't remember his name, really, only his arm. The guy was a flamethrower. Just watching him take a few warm-up tosses was enough to scare me spitless.

I remembered the coach's instruction about being aggressive at the plate. And so, as I stepped into the batter's box, I tried to dig in—to hunker down. And then I heard a voice. Behind me. A voice I recognized. It was my grandad, cheering for me. As I readied myself to hit, he told the whole crowd listening that if I hit a home run, he would give me the brand-new silver dollar he had in his pocket.

I tried. With all my might, I wanted to hit that ball, but it came right at my head. I ducked. It curved. At the very last possible moment it curved and caught the edge of home plate. Three times I ducked. Three times it curved. "Yer out!" declared the umpire. And the crowd of locals cheered their team; they screamed and clapped because I had struck out, a standing ovation in the midst of my failure.

And then it was time to go home.

I have total recall about how I felt that day, walking away from home plate. Inadequate and embarrassed are two words that come to mind. I had let my team down, my family down, my grandad down. I got in the game for only a short while. I was not a key player. But somehow, I still felt totally responsible. I know now, of course, that that was not true. But I did not know it then.

And I never told another soul how I felt on the long ride home from Eminence. Over the years, I put it out of my mind and just forgot all about it.

But last fall in the Oakland Coliseum on a warm Saturday evening, I sat with nearly fifty thousand other men singing and listening at a Promise Keepers rally. They called the pastors in the huge crowd to climb down from their seats in the stands and make their way onto the playing field. A thunderous ovation began. I left my bench seat and joined thousands of my pastor brothers on the outfield grass. For nearly fifteen minutes, men stood and screamed and cheered encouragement to pastors they did not even know. They did not know which of us were great preachers and which of us weren't all that great, which of us could write and which of us couldn't. They had no clue which of us pastored large churches and which of us pastored small flocks. They did not know. They did not care. They only expressed love.

As I stood on that field, I became aware, again, of the importance of encouraging one another in The Climb. Looking up toward the face of a God I knew and fifty thousand men I had never met, my emotion overcame me and I wept. Humbled. Privileged to be called "pastor." Insignificant, really, except for Jesus. But the ovation and expression of support and understanding overcame, for the moment at least, my feelings of inadequacy and the shortcomings and failures and frailties I carry with me every day.

I know it may sound strange to you, but it is true. Believe me, it is true. I remember thinking to myself . . . about how different that ballpark was from the one in Eminence, and how different the ovation was from the one he received on his climb toward Jerusalem.

Only five days remained before Jesus would die. I can't say what he felt that Sunday morning he awoke. We do know he had just spent the night in Bethany, and now he prepared for a short, triumphant journey into Jerusalem, the city of David. He must have felt something. It must have seemed in some strange way like he was going home. Dual citizenship, perhaps. He wasn't headed toward his hometown, of course. Everyone knows he was born in Bethlehem, of the seed and lineage of Jesse, of the seed and lineage of David. And everyone knows he was raised in Nazareth—Jesus, the son of Joseph, Jesus, the Son of God. But in just a few hours now, he would return once more to the city of his fathers.

The holy city is not far from Bethany, where he spent the previous night, about a mile and a half. Certainly not a long walk. But prophecy must be fulfilled, and so the Lord gave instructions to his disciples. "Go to the village ahead of you, and just as you enter it you will find a colt tied there which no one has ever ridden. Untie it and bring it here. If anyone asks you, 'Why are you doing this?' tell him, 'The Lord needs it, and will send it back shortly.'"

When the disciples arrived back with the colt, they threw their cloaks over it. And then, it was time. Time for another climb. The Savior climbed atop the colt's back, and began his ascent toward Jerusalem. A mountain of adulation began to rise before him. Green fields along the way were lined with palms, and the people plucked the branches and began waving them before the rabbi. Some cast them down in the road before his colt, the fronds falling from adoring hands into a thatched green carpet. The Son was out, the warmth of his light evident.

The mountains wanted to applaud; the rocks could have cried out. But there was no need for nature to join in. The people would shout their affirmation and praise, with voices loud and significant.

"Blessed is the King, who comes in the name of the Lord! Peace in heaven and glory in the highest."

And still he rode on toward Jerusalem, following a triumphant path, softened with the cloaks of men and the fickle adulation of the crowds.

The sandy dirt along the road must have elicited a certain ancient and intense sense of identity deep within him. He belonged to this place, and this place belonged to him. Here was lineage. Family ties. The Root of Jesse approaching the city of David.

Jesus, the Anointed One, pointed his face toward this august place of eminence, heritage, and tradition: Jerusalem. He wept when he saw her. He was broken for her. And yet, he would soon be broken by her.

When his entourage reached the city, intense questions swirled among the people and stirred them to ask who he was. But the Lord of heaven and earth knew his family ties beckoned him not only to David's city but to his Father's business as well.

"Out of control—the whole world is in a stampede after him," said the Pharisees, eyeing the adulation.

"Wait awhile, and see," said the devil. For he knew that five days later, the stampede would slow and stop . . . at the foot of Skull Hill.

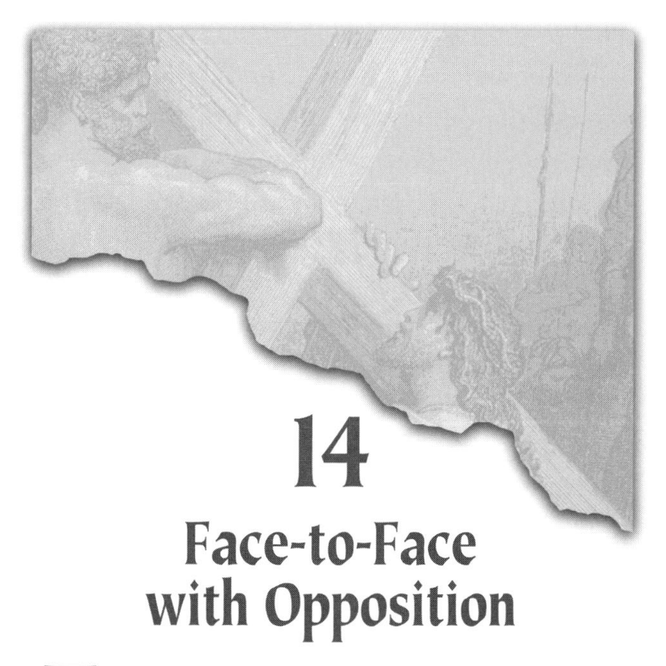

14
Face-to-Face with Opposition

I have a hunch there's a nationwide test given to people applying for jobs in the planning department or the building permit department of every city or county government in this country, standardized for easy grading. It's an aptitude test. It's a secret test, too. It must be. I've never seen a copy of it, and those who have taken it never divulge its contents. Sworn to secrecy, I suppose.

And the first question on that test, after name, address, and phone is this one: "What were the first words you ever spoke?"

If the answer is "mom-ma" or "dad-dee," then you flunk. You don't get to be a planner or an inspector.

If your first words were, "No, you can't do that; you don't have the right permit or permission or proper zoning," then they move you to the front of the line. You're a prime candidate for being either a county or city planner, or a building inspector. I may sound jaded, and you may suspect there is more to my vexation than is immediately on the surface. You are right. Building inspectors and planning commissions drive me nuts. I will tell you about it.

I don't know how the building permit department in your community works, but I have been involved in more than a few building projects over the past several years of ministry in various communities across the country. The one thing I have learned from governmental agencies, and especially building departments, is this: If you're planning on building something, all roads lead through "building" and "planning." And the first answer to every question or request put to them—no matter how large or small the community—is always the same: "No. You can't do that here."

I'm not sure what makes them so disagreeable. They either want you to abandon your plans altogether, or at the very least modify them so tremendously that any semblance between what you had originally planned and what they have planned for you is purely coincidental.

Several years ago, a church I served here in California as a young associate pastor was involved in a building project. All our plans had been approved—finally—by the city planners. (I will not tell you which city, in case I end up there again sometime, and find myself wishing I had been more discreet in my disclosures.) One day my pastor asked me to meet a building inspector at our construction site and get a signature on the nail inspection for our drywall. The inspector had to come and verify that we had enough nails in the drywall before they covered it with "mud" and tape.

I met the inspector at the appointed time and did not anticipate any difficulty getting his signature on our permit. But as he ambled around our new church building site, I noticed that he walked with a certain Napoleonic swagger, looking with disdain at our volunteer nail job. He turned up his mouth on one side, smirking as he looked over our job. *Why does he need to shake his head?* I wondered. *Was that something they teach you or is it "factory" installed at birth?* I did not know nor care. I only wanted my permit signed.

I thought I would take a congenial approach and chat casually with the obviously negative man. "We sure are proud of our building. We have people coming every night after work to help us. And we're making good progress, too. That drywall is going right on up, isn't it?" I asked, wanting to include him and make this civil servant feel welcome in our new church building.

But he did not act welcomed. In fact, he did not even act civil. "Yeah, I see your drywall is going right on up, but will it stay up? That's my question."

Will it stay up? Was that rhetorical? Was I supposed to answer? Well, I did. Impetuosity blurted out words that hadn't been thought through. Without hesitation, I told him I guaranteed it would stay up. I quoted Jesus. "The Bible says, 'Upon this rock I will build my church and the gates of hell will not prevail against it.' That's good enough for me." I do not think he noticed that I quoted the verse out of context. He didn't mention it, at least. Nor that my verse had nothing whatever to do with construction or drywall.

He just grabbed the posted permit and initialed it in the appropriate spot and then walked away, mumbling to himself. I do not know why.

After completing our building, our volunteer workers began on the parking lot. The pastoral staff was the first line of the team. The senior pastor and I went out and started knocking out the sidewalk one day and clearing the way for the big bulldozers coming in soon to begin paving preparations. We worked all week long. Our final task included digging around the roots of a tree that needed removal because it stood smack in the center of what would be the entrance to our property. Because we had the permits approved for our parking lot, we thought it would be all right with local officials if we removed the tree.

We thought wrong.

As we started working on the tree, a city inspector and a worker from the tree division of the parks and recreation department happened by and saw us hacking on that tree. Immediately they stopped and issued a "cease and desist" order. It was verbal, but very authoritarian just the same.

"This tree cannot be removed without specific authorization and proper signatures," they said. "You gotta have a yellow sticker on this tree before you can take it down."

My senior pastor explained that we did have permission to do what we were doing, and referred them to the plans already approved by the city planners. Then he added these words: "I don't have time for a sticker. The bulldozer will be here tomorrow."

But the inspector and city worker would not budge. The result was a deadlock between the city and the church. A close encounter of the worst kind. My pastor was messing with their rules and regulations. And so the threat.

"If you don't stop right now, we'll have you arrested," said one of the men in an angry tone.

"I understand," said my kind and gentle pastor. "You have to do what you have to do. And we have to do what we have to do. There's a bulldozer coming here first thing tomorrow morning to begin grading for our parking lot, and this tree stands in the way of progress. It must be removed. If you have to have us arrested, then I guess we'll be arrested."

And he went back to cutting at the roots as the two men walked back to their car to radio for police to come and arrest two blatant felons. I did not know what to do. This man was my mentor, my teacher, my friend. I could not imagine that he was prepared to "die" on this seemingly insignificant mountain.

I continued to press him to stop and at least call the architect for his opinion before we both were carted off to jail. I was, after all, a young man. He was older and had most of his ministry behind him. How could I explain a criminal record on my résumé to churches that might be interested in my ministry? He finally agreed and went inside to make a quick call. He learned from the architect that getting a yellow sticker for our tree was only a minor formality. Within a day or so they would have to let us go ahead and take out the tree. Maybe the best thing would be to wait.

We did wait. But we didn't have to wait very long. The next morning when the bulldozer arrived, I guess its operator hadn't gotten the memo on waiting. He saw that tree sitting smack in the middle of where it wasn't supposed to be and assumed it needed to be displaced. And so, he just moved it;

he slipped the blade of his front-loading bucket under it and pushed it—roots and all—over into the corner of our lot.

And that, as they say, was the end of that. By the time the yellow sticker finally came, the limbs on the tree for which it was intended were as brittle as broom straw and dead as the leaves of fall.

So what's the point? Just this.

There are lots of things that get me going. Government bureaucracy with its red tape is one of them. And I may chafe at it, complain about it, and disagree with it. But I'm not going to die on that insignificant mountain. I understand that we need to work within the system and that planners and inspectors are here to help us all. I hope you could tell by my tongue-in-cheek humor that my distaste for governmental bureaucracy isn't terminal. I may get a little exasperated now and then with the red tape. "Pushed," my wife calls it. But I'm not willing to die on that mountain.

But the fact that I am not willing to die on *that* mountain does not mean that I am not willing to die on *any* mountain. Commitment to The Climb demands that we get more than "pushed" when irreconcilable differences exist between our faith and structures and institutions that stand in opposition to God's plan. Passionless Christianity will never produce opposition, but if we are committed to The Climb, the path to the final summit surely travels up the mountain of opposition. And if you need a primer course on the kinds of things that ought to shake us up, check out the last five days he spent in the face of Jerusalem's spiritual elite.

It didn't take him long to come face-to-face with the opposition. Less than one day, really. On Sunday, cheering people welcomed him to the community. But on Monday morning, the cheers changed to jeers.

It all had started innocently enough. Jesus entered the city and made his way toward the temple, a house of prayer. But as he approached, a certain distasteful sound greeted him. A bitter sound, not of men crying out to their God, asking for a change of heart; instead, his ears were assaulted by the sound of men crying out for another kind of change—exact change. Money changers lined the sides of the temple court area, and the sound of their commerce ignited a holy indignation in the Lamb of God.

Money changers had become a regular part of the temple life. The law of Moses required that when the Jewish nation was numbered, every male Israelite who was twenty years or older had to pay into the temple treasury a half-shekel as an offering to the Lord (Exod. 30:13–15). This had to be paid by using the exact Hebrew half-shekel, and the money changers provided the right coins for the multitudes that came to Jerusalem for the feasts.

But the money dealers didn't assist people without financial gain of their own; they charged a "small" transaction fee of 12 percent. And in addition to meeting the need for the half-shekel tribute money, the money changers provided the exact coins necessary to purchase the animals or doves required in the sacrifices for the temple, but again, at tremendous fee rates.

For some people, money changing represented a legitimate business, but the high interest rates and the sound of money that filled the temple courts enraged Jesus. The racket of loose coins rang in the ears of God. The Lion of Judah had heard and seen enough. Time to rearrange people's thinking. Time to turn the tables on the money mongers.

"My house shall be called a house of prayer, but you've made it a den of robbers," stormed the Lord of the winds. And now, the temple was filled with the sound of filthy lucre bouncing on the ground and rolling out the door of God's house of prayer—loose change for sure.

The chief priests and the teachers of the law, of course, took umbrage at this interloper Jesus edging in on their turf. They were making good money in the temple courts; how dare he say it was bad. Who did he think he was, anyway? God?

Like mob bosses, these temple racketeers put out a contract on Jesus. It must be done with discretion, because the people were still hanging on his every word, but the religious leaders and chief priests had come to a decision: Jesus must die.

On Tuesday, his commitment took him back into the city. Again, he knew the challenge of The Climb—a growing mountain of opposition. His authority was being questioned, it seemed. At every ministry venue, those who wanted to trip him up and impede the progress of the kingdom posed questions and challenged his right to set himself up as some kind of expert on God. "Who gives you the authority to do what you're doing?" the leaders asked. But he continued hacking at the very roots of their system and the way they approached righteousness. He pronounced judgment on their hollow rules and regulations. Without permit. Without permission, the Good Shepherd made a public nuisance of himself. He spoke up. He spoke out. He railed against injustice and mediocrity. Impassioned. Abrasive. Anything but Milquetoast.

Facing Jesus in public was, of course, no picnic for the religious leaders. The people thronged around him to hear his words. If the chief priests were going to be successful, they'd have to trick him, spy on him, perhaps, with well-placed informants. They sent honest-looking men with innocent-sounding questions to the Innocent One. If they could somehow get Jesus to admit that he opposed governments and civil authority, then they could have Governor Pilate do their dirty work and kill him. Taxes usually incite strong emotions in governors. They would try to trick Jesus with a question about taxes.

"Is it right," they asked, "for us to pay taxes to Caesar or not? Should we pay or shouldn't we?" A tricky question, indeed. If he preached against paying taxes, they would have grounds to haul him before Pilate. And if he supported the heavy taxes of Caesar, the people would revolt against him because he favored suppressing the people with unreasonable financial hardships. Imagine the depth of their folly, trying to put the Rock of Ages between a rock and a hard place. Their duplicity did not tax his divine wisdom in the least.

"Show me a coin," said the Holy One. And now, he asked simple questions of his own. Whose picture and inscription were on the coin? "Caesar's," they replied.

And then, he astonished them. He answered their hard question with a very simple answer: "Give Caesar what is his; give God what is his." What's so hard about that?

No wonder he had such a difficult time with "ecclesiastical city hall." He looked straight at the "religious ones" and called them names—vipers, hypocrites, whitewashed tombs that look good on the outside, but on the inside are full of dead men's bones.

Interestingly, on the final days before his arrest, Jesus inspected mighty edifices, buildings made with the hands of men. The stone the builders rejected walked among them, predicting that not one stone would go unturned.

And all the while, the demons of hell plotted and planned his death, counting the spikes, and wondering how many nails it would eventually take to finally pin down the Truth.

15
The Climb to the Second Story

I'm the oldest child in my family. My brother Dan is eighteen months younger than me. My sister, Candy, is four years younger than me. And then, there is my little brother, Todd. He's younger than me, too—more than twenty years younger. That's right. One night at the supper table just after my twentieth birthday, my folks announced that Mom was "great with child." Amazing. When Todd came along, we were thrilled, and enjoyed having a baby in the family. He's still the baby, and always will be.

It's probably an hour's drive from Granite City to an amusement park on the outskirts of St. Louis called Six Flags over Mid-America. When my little brother Todd was eight or nine, I took him there. Television commercials had been airing for weeks in our area, trying to lure patrons and convince people that Six Flags would be a great way to spend a day. Some of the TV spots depicted smiling people watching musical productions and eating fattening foods, little kids sitting on merry-go-rounds, fast-paced shots of theme park mascots waving and motioning for people to "come join the fun."

But those weren't the spots that finally convinced us. One commercial was different from all the rest; it grabbed our attention and convinced us we had to go to Six Flags. It featured shots of people riding a roller coaster called the Screamin' Eagle. The announcer said the ride was so high and so fast that it would "take your breath away—maybe for good!" My little brother and I just *had* to check it out.

Three words best describe our experience that day as we rode the Screamin' Eagle—*out of control*. The commercial didn't lie; it had a speed so severe and vertical drops so steep that the entire ride felt like an out-of-control fall off a mountain bike. Planned terror, I suppose you could call it.

People board that roller coaster knowing full well what they're in for. Standing in line for forty-five minutes before you get your turn lets you see train after train of people leave the loading platform—macho guys, looking like they may read a book or visit with a friend while they're on the ride, ebullient young girls, smiling and laughing, some of them so nonchalant they look like they might break out their polish and start doing their nails any second. Cool customers.

But that's before their ride.

Two minutes later, the train comes back. Now, the guys look "pressed down, shaken together, and running over" (if you get my drift). Eyes wide as headlights on high beam. And the gals look blown and unkempt, holding on to the bars in front of them with the grips of lady wrestlers. I guess that's where they got the name for the Screamin' Eagle. Some of those girls started screaming when they got on the train and didn't stop until they got off.

I think the thing that got to me most when I rode that coaster was how slowly it pulled away from the loading platform. I've had faster escalator rides than that. No hint of what was ahead. Up. Up. The roller coaster crawled to incredible heights before it reached a brief and pointless summit; then, before acclimation to such altitudes could be achieved, a plummet at breakneck speed—straight down. The first drop compressed my lungs so intensely that I expected one of those yellow oxygen masks that look like margarine cups to pop up for passenger use. And for the next two minutes or so, I was jerked and slammed and raced around a track so quickly I didn't really have time to recover from one banked turn until the next one whipped my body in the opposite direction.

Fun. Terror. Amusement? I guess so.

Roller coasters come in a lot of shapes and forms. Sometimes, they take a high and twisting track; sturdy wooden beams and frames rise beneath them to give safety and structure and stability. Sometimes they run through water. Sometimes over the tops of pretend mountains. Their height makes them visible from afar, and the sounds of distant laughter and screams of thrill and delight add to their mystique and adventure. People stand in long lines and pay serious money for the thrill of riding those kinds of roller coasters. But one thing everyone knows about roller coasters. If you get on . . . sooner or later, you will get off.

Not necessarily, though. Whether you get to get off or not depends on what kind of roller coaster you're on.

Emotional roller coasters are different from any ride at an amusement park. Emotional roller coasters sneak up on you. You can't anticipate them. No warning about their ominous beginnings. They just show up. No one in their right mind would want to ride an emotional roller coaster. People don't pay money to get on. In fact, they'd give anything they have just to be able to get off, to get away from the bobbing and weaving and fear. There's a certain sick feeling in the gut of the soul of someone on that kind of roller coaster. It's a pain, but not one that aspirin can help. A nausea that stomach remedies won't cure. Motion sickness best describes it, I guess. A desperate condition caused by unexpected mountains and unpredicted storms. A sickness of soul. A heaving of life's waves, buffeting and battering, and the suddenness of a storm, unexpected and violent, which will not be calmed. No, people don't choose to get on those kinds of roller coasters. As soon as they detect what's going on, they want to get off.

But they can't. Circumstances beyond their control dictate what comes next, and it seems like the ride will never end.

Over the course of writing this book, I've known some of that kind of roller coaster experience. I've already mentioned my dad's surgery. But what I haven't mentioned yet is what the rest of the last few months have looked like.

You see, my mom had surgery, too. In fact, it was just a few weeks after my dad's surgery. She had an aneurysm. Her heart condition made surgery extremely serious. Another trip for me across the country. Another roller coaster ride with my little brother, Todd, as we sat side by side. We had no idea how long it would take or when it would end. Doctors finally told us that the surgery was over; they had almost lost her on the table. The next few days would be critical. More nights of waiting in hospital rooms and days of drinking that horrible hospital coffee. But she's mending now.

Before my mom had really recovered from her surgery, Randee had major surgery. My wife suffered from chronic pain for most of our married life, and she had surgery to help alleviate some of those problems. I waited in a hospital again, this time during a five-hour surgery in San Francisco.

Randee's mom had major surgery, too. Can you believe it? Within seven days of my wife's surgery, my mother-in-law underwent a difficult procedure, with weeks of painful convalescence.

Four major surgeries in my family in less than seven months. What an emotional roller coaster.

But it wasn't time to get off yet.

You see, there was still Gary. He's my friend and a great missionary. We've been best friends for almost thirty years. We've traveled thousands of miles together on ministry trips, from Europe to Central America. We served on the same staff for many years. Our relationship is not one of those sickeningly sweet, sentimental things. It's deep and genuine, and it's terribly important to me. I depend on him; he depends on me. He is, quite simply, my dear brother in Christ.

Several months ago, my friend Gary discovered a lump on the side of his neck that began to bother him. After some coaxing from his wife, he went to the doctor. Two appointments later, they finally did tests and removed the lump. Cancer. The specific name the doctors gave it was non-Hodgkin's lymphoma. Within one week of being told my dad had cancer, my best friend of nearly thirty years sat down in my office to say, "Sorry your dad's got cancer; oh, and by the way, so do I."

If there is such a thing as a cancer-related pain—and I believe there is—it reached across the table between us that very moment and grabbed at my gut. I could hardly handle my despair.

Chemotherapy began immediately for Gary. I went with him a couple of times to those appointments. And I sat again, waiting . . . this time, for my friend. After six months of chemotherapy treatments, doctors have pronounced him cancer-free.

Over those past seven or eight months, with my Dad and Gary and with my mom and Randee, I felt like I'd been on an incredible emotional roller coaster. I've had all the ups and downs I care to have for a while. But you know what? I didn't get a choice. And neither do you. God—our wise, loving God—can permit them at any moment.

I am confident that as I told you about my last few months of roller coaster life, you thought about your own miseries and challenges and "yucky stuff." Some of you who read these words know a pain or disappointment far deeper than I have ever experienced. Troubled kids or broken marriages.

Homosexuality or chronic illness. Sudden deaths. Histories strewn with abuse and violence. When those times come, maybe you've been tempted to ask the same question I have.

In the midst of my own personal pain, in the midst of the struggle, in the midst of The Climb, there is a question that occurred to me more than once during the last several months.

It was a "why" question. Not, "Why is this happening to me?" (Believe me, I wondered about that, but I never asked.) I didn't ask "Why does *everything* seem to be happening to us?" either, though during the past several months it seemed that everything was happening to me, my family, or my friends.

But one day, in the midst of a particularly sober pity party, I struggled with the unrelenting nature of The Climb. I decided to ask God to answer the "why" question you may have wondered about, too.

Shortly after I started writing this book on The Climb . . . shortly after I learned of my friend's lymphoma, I decided to ask.

I wanted an answer to the question of why God didn't do something about all of this.

But then, it occurred to me: *He did. He did do something . . .*

Thursday night, Passover. Only a few more hours until the terror would begin. Then love would compel the Master to step into death's chasm. Time was of the essence. And the Savior's desire to savor every remaining moment with his own led him to take them to an isolated upper room. Slow and deliberate, up narrow steps to a large, open room on a second story.

The Passover meal sat on the table ready to be eaten. Time to show and tell. Time to demonstrate the full extent of his love.

And so, the Savior took off his outer clothing. Uncovered. Unashamed and without guile. He who once wore swaddling clothes now donned another brief and humble garment: a servant's towel wrapped tight around his waist. And then the sound. What was that sound? Water? Water, indeed. Splashing into a basin, splashing on disciples' feet. Holy vessel and Water of Life touching men.

But what of the betrayer, Judas, the thief and devil's interloper? Why was he allowed to sit and watch this act of goodness and mercy? He would leave soon enough, but not before water—wet as bitter tears—flowed over his guilty feet, too.

"Do you understand?" he asked them all. Lord and Teacher stooping to model The Climb. So many dirty feet, washed by one who truly cared. The Teacher continued to demonstrate the only way to be truly blessed: servanthood.

And now, time for the Passover Lamb to share the lamb of Passover, the bitter herbs, and the unleavened bread.

"I have eagerly desired to eat with you before I suffer," he said. And he took the bread, gave thanks, and said, "My body, broken for you . . . remember." And he took the cup in like manner, and said, "A new covenant . . . my blood, poured out for you . . . remember." But they did not understand. Even in this upper room, even at this solemn time, arguments arose among the disciples about which of them was considered the greatest.

They sat for several more moments, listening to the Master. Some of them boasted about their willingness to go to prison with him or die with him. But no one mentioned how much fun it would be to serve with him, and wash feet with him. More teaching. More discussion. More friendship.

And then it was time to leave. Time for the Man of Sorrows to become acquainted with grief.

A haunting melody began; a song arose before they went out.

Extraordinary note of irony.

The entire company singing a hymn . . . about him.

16

Final Assault on the Summit

If you call my house tonight and want to talk to me, you'd better call before eight-thirty or so, California time. If you haven't called by then, you won't get me. You may talk to my wife; you might get to talk to one of my sons. But I can almost guarantee I won't be available. More than likely, I'll be asleep.

My family teases me because they say I don't fall asleep, I fall into a deep sinkhole of unconsciousness. Even if I try to stay awake during some movie they want me to watch with them, it's difficult for me to keep my eyes open. Just too sleepy in the evenings. But since I get to bed early, I get up early, too. In fact, my favorite part of the day is from five until seven or so in the morning.

I never need an alarm clock; I've got one in my head. I wake up every morning about four-thirty, and as soon as I open my eyes, I know—I just know that God has been up for hours waiting for someone to talk to. Might as well be me.

Besides, *he* always lets me know it's time to get up anyway; Chanticleer, I mean. That may not be his real name, but it's what I call him. Someone in our neighborhood owns a rooster. I haven't been able to locate exactly which yard he lives in, but I wait for his plaintive "Er'-rr, Er'-rr, Errrrr!" every morning just before dawn and then, my feet hit the floor.

I usually follow the same routine; it varies only if I have an early morning appointment. I shower and shave first. Then, I walk downstairs and start a pot of coffee. When it's finished perking, I pour myself a mug, and put the rest into an insulated decanter. Then, I take the decanter and my coffee mug and go back upstairs to my office. I sit down at my desk. I take out my favorite pen (a beautiful, jet-black fountain pen with an extra broad tip that my friend Roger Mahany gave me) and I open two books. One is my journal, the other, my Bible. I print the date, the day, and the time in my journal, and then I close it momentarily. I open my Bible, and I read.

I do not read a predetermined number of verses or chapters. I read until I sense God's Word has spoken to me. That may take nine verses, or nine chapters. No matter, either way. I read until God's Word has spoken to me. Then, I open my journal again. I print one or two of the verses I just read, and then I write a short piece in my journal.

Sometimes my journal writings reflect inner struggles; sometimes they depict happenings in my day. But always, they revolve around what Christ means to me. The last thing I do is pray for my wife, my kids, and other special concerns I may have.

Each of us needs a secret place where we can go to write and think and pray, a room whose walls will hear our groanings to him. The demands of The Climb necessitate that there be at least one place where we can always be free to express our fears or insecurities without feeling like someone will be looking over our shoulder. For me, that place is upstairs in my office; it is inside the pages of my journal.

For him, it was a secluded spot near the Mount of Olives.

The Sinkhole

A strange quiet pervaded the halls of heaven as the angelic hosts watched the Prince of Peace leave that upper room to finish The Climb. Down the steps, down silent streets that would soon echo with taunts and jeers. The entourage of disciples followed the Master; they walked in the cool night air. They made their way toward a place they all knew well, a favorite meeting place near the foot of the Mount of Olives, a garden-like enclosure called Gethsemane, which means *press of oils.*

And God the Father watched it all in silence.

When they reached Gethsemane, Jesus instructed eight of his disciples to wait for him near the entrance to the garden while he went farther inside to pray. But he extended a personal invitation to three who seemed to be his closest friends: Peter (who, moments before had said he would never deny him), and the brothers James and John. These three would have the honor of watching with the Lord during the last visitation he would have with the Father . . . before it was time. Four men walked into the face of agony, though only One of them really recognized the awfulness of it all.

As the angels watched in sadness, they noticed an anguish in the stride of the Prince. Here was a gait they had never seen before, a heaviness of heart and step. The weariness and weight of The Climb nearly buckled his knees now, as he made his way toward that place of prayer.

"Look, holy Lord," said one of the angels. "The Righteous One agonizes in distress and trouble."

And that was so. Jesus paused to tell his three friends of the overwhelming anguish of spirit and sadness in his soul, a pain so severe in his sacred heart that he sorrowed nearly "to the point of death."

And then, the needy man's request. "Stay here and keep watch with me," Jesus asked his three sleepy friends.

And he climbed . . . into a sinkhole of agony. He knelt to pray. Darkness and despair awaited him and swallowed him whole and holy and alive. The pending aloneness and separation from the Father wilted his flesh; fear pummeled his spirit. And love introduced the will of an obedient Son to the will of a righteous God. Never had there been such a meeting of wills. Jesus wept.

"Father," cried the Son, "If you are willing, take this cup from me!" And the angels heard the request of the only child of God. And the demons of hell heard it too; they listened to that same pitiful cry. Such a bitter cup, such a dread-filled cup of agony. But they only teased and taunted. They hoped for the ultimate sinking—that the Messiah, the Anointed One, would renounce his mission.

"Yes," screamed the hordes of hell. "Beg and plead with your Father; perhaps you will convince him to take the cup from your weak and trembling hand." *The servant, the fool, will fall into the sinkhole and die,* they told themselves. *He will lose in vain obedience to his Father. Ha!* And then they began a dance without music.

> In hell there is no music—
> an agonizing night that never ends
> as songless as a shattered violin[1]

But, the man of sorrows spoke again. "Not what I will, Father. Your will . . ." And he sobbed and wept.

Every member of heaven's host stood, hoping the Father would send one of them to comfort the Prince. And it was so. The Father nodded to one of the angels, and immediately he went to the Son's aid and strengthened him, enabling him to continue his vigil. More than an hour Jesus prayed.

His three friends struggled with sorrow, too. But their exhaustion in the face of The Climb finally overtook them. They slept. Three times he awoke them from a weary sleep. Three times in the midst of The Climb, about to approach the summit, they slumbered. Asleep on the darkest night that ever was.

When they finally awoke, it was time for all four to face the strange noise—a dirge of soldiers and an orchestrated betrayal. And the sinkhole continued to deepen all night long.

Judas brought a revealing kiss for his Lord.

And guards dragged the Lamb away.

And the disciples fled.

And Peter stood by a warming fire, dodging questions, avoiding answers, cussing like a sailor.

And then, the night was over, and a sound split the quiet dawn.

"Er'-rr, Er'-rr, Errrrr!" A rooster greeted the morning . . . for the third time.

The Climb to Skull Hill

So many eloquent and stirring things have been written over the years about the blessed Savior's climb up the steep path to Golgotha. As I approach the solemn scene of crucifixion in my mind, I doubt my own ability to tell you more than you already know. The best description, of course, was written by God himself in his Word.

The Gospels tell the story. Inspired writers recorded the sights and sounds—sounds we cannot hear because they are described with mere words, and yet sounds just the same. An audio reminder on four Gospel tracks, contrapuntal and plain as black and white. A collage of words in stereo, an accurate recording so all would know of those awful sounds.

The echoes of mocking laughter. The thud of fists striking that holy face, and the sound of spittle hurled from foul mouths. Shouts of the angry mob. The snap of whip against flesh, and the screams of Mary's oldest son.

Stripped and wearing only his undergarment, the Son of Man carries the cross beam into the streets of lost men and lives. He bears his load alone to Skull Hill. The heavy timber echoes as he drags it over cobblestones. And then, a sorry sound, as the sorrowed man stumbles. Then, a compelling sound: Simon of Cyrene, pressed into duty. As the pitiful entourage approaches the summit, the cries of two guilty thieves split the air.

And now, the decibels rise as he approaches the finale of The Climb. The sobs of a weeping mother. The ping of hammer striking nail. The sound of nails piercing palms. The ring of sin's toll, a pealing to announce that the hour had finally come. The sound of innocence rising and writhing in pain. Innocence being slain. And the sound of planting—a rugged cross, buried to its roots.

And the voice of the Man-child calling for his daddy.

And the silence of a daddy who did not answer.

The Climb That Could Never Be

The enemy grew bold, seeing that sin had fastened him fast and secure to those rough-hewn timbers. Pain and agony had now taken up permanent residence in the fleshly temple of Jesus, and Satan delighted in those bleeding hands and feet. That ridiculous crown amused him immensely; the thorny one that was too small for his royal head and had to be mashed over his brow.

"Perfect fit," scoffed the evil one. "This Lion King seems to have lost his roar."

The demons of hell had left their lairs to come and enjoy the view, too, each taking a turn at adding insult to the injury of God in the flesh. "No overturned temple tables, now," they sneered. "We don't hear angels singing, either."

Perhaps it was time for one, final try. The spikes in his hands and feet made The Climb nigh impossible now. The dark one prepared one final challenge he hoped would persuade the King of the Jews to give up one climb for another.

One last try at coaxing "self" out of the Selfless One.

"If you're really God's Son, climb down from that cross. It would be so easy for a God like you. It would only take a moment, and all this tragedy would be finished," said the liar, lying in wait.

Earth paused. Heaven waited. The entire universe held its collective breath to see what the Savior would say. But the Holy One was too committed to The Climb; love compelled him to stay where he was. He would never betray the Father's plan.

When the Lamb finally rejected climbing down from the summit, the disgusted enemy pronounced a mocking retort: "Did you know you're a miserable excuse for man?"

As some of the onlookers conveyed the taunts in human form—"Let this Christ, this King of Israel, come down now from the cross, that we may see and believe"—bold ghouls nestled on the Savior's dislocated shoulders and began to mock him. "Have you noticed how dark the day has grown? Even the sun refused to get up this morning. You're all alone, you know. The whole world has abandoned you; they've turned against the Light of the World."

"Yes," said another imp who laughed at the Prince from beneath his cross. "It's the darkest noon we can ever remember."

Then Satan himself rubbed salt into the Prince's wound. "Has anyone seen your daddy? Even he didn't come to see about you, did he?"

And the tormented Savior finally screamed, his voice piercing the darkness of that day: "My God, my God. Why have you forsaken me?"

No answer came.

And Satan laughed, and said, "See? Even God is at a loss for words."

The harmless Lamb hung suspended and gasping for breath . . . until the ninth hour.

Then, he pronounced that it was finished, and passed his spirit back into the Father's caring hands.

> And he hung his head for the shame of it all . . . and he died.

17
Requiem

And having knelt, God groaned and bore me my second time. In pain, I was born in a rain of godly blood: blood that I had caused, for I burst my God, the brow and the palms and the heart of God, in order to be born; but blood my God did not begrudge me, for this was the very life of God upon me.

"Wash me! Wash me clean."[1]

Once a Man hung on a tree;
Innocent, between two thieves.
  Who is this Man, with bloodstained brow,
    Who 'though he dies, still lives, somehow?
Who is this Man, with arms outstretched in love?

Drops of blood fall to the ground,
As, through the air, a plaintive sound;
    "Forgive them, Father, I beg you.
        They really don't know what they do."
Who is this Man, who speaks such words of love?

Seldom do you hear his name,
And only then by men in vain.
    They slander One who died for all;
        They mock his love; ignore the call
Of him, whose arms are still outstretched in love.

How unfair, it seems to me,
That One should die on such a tree,
    And then have those for whom he died,
        Just turn their backs, and close their eyes
To him, whose voice still speaks such words of love.

Who is this Man?

His name is Wonderful . . . Counselor . . .
Prince of Peace, is he.

Bread of Life . . . Living Water . . .
Light, that men might see.

Ever-living Savior . . . Lord . . .
And one day, coming King.

His name is Jesus . . .
Jesus . . .
    Jesus Christ . . .
    the King.

18

The Day the Word Got Out

I don't know where I heard it first. But for as long as I can remember, I have known it. There are two kinds of people who may profess to be Christians: the "talkin' kind" and the "walkin' kind." It's one thing to memorize John 3:16; it's quite another to be committed to The Climb. He never intended to issue a call of convenience, but rather sacrifice, conviction, and exciting challenge. The early followers of Christ discovered that truth the morning they approached the empty hole in the ground, the hole they thought was his tomb. But the disciples weren't the only ones who were surprised.

Hell smirked and laughed and guffawed, too. The demons must have been amused that caring friends laid him in a borrowed tomb. But Satan made one huge mistake. He misunderstood. He thought, "It is finished!" meant it was finished. As cunning and crafty as he was, he must have left his dictionary or thesaurus on the shelf. He didn't understand the full meaning of the living Word. *Immortal* means *death-proof*.

By Sunday morning, the living Stone had rolled smack through the gates of hell. In spite of all the enemy could do, the Word got out! And when Mary showed up to anoint the body of the Lord, she discovered the Door, open for kingdom business! And the aroma of Christ spread like a holy perfume throughout that part of the world.

That first Easter morning when the disciples discovered the resurrection, they weren't the only ones who noticed. Government officials gave a look, too. They peeked inside that gaping hole—the one that had been "death-proofed" by Immanuel—and pronounced that he was gone, all right. *Must have been stolen sometime in the night. Or maybe he wasn't dead when we put him in there, after all. Maybe he revived on that cold slab of stone and pushed that two-ton rock away all by himself.*

No matter, either way. The officials were perfectly willing to let his harmless followers believe whatever they wished, as long as they didn't interfere with governments and institutions. They were done with him.

Well, governments and institutions may have been done with him, but he wasn't done with them. Those early Christians were actually convinced that Jesus was alive. That's why they were called "believers." Christ appeared to several of his friends over the course of forty days after the resurrection. He ate with his disciples; he mended Peter's broken promises and cleared up Thomas's doubts. He climbed another mountain with them in Galilee and gave his climbing companions a simple instruction: "Go . . . make disciples."

And then he climbed one final time. He ascended to the right hand of the Father and took his rightful place. But his words—his final words to them as he was leaving—kept ringing in their ears: "I will be with you always, to the very end of the age."

From that time on, there was no such thing as "church as usual." He gave a once-and-for-all call to radical belief. Not the "talkin' kind" of religious jargon they had always heard, but the "walkin' kind" of commitment to The Climb that would change the world. And he—the Risen One who had been dead but was now alive forevermore—would continue to lead the way.

He ascended to heaven, and those young believers had an innocent prayer meeting in an upper room. But it was not church as usual. God sent them power, when he blew their cover. A holy wind came up. A holy fire fell. And the river of the Holy Spirit completely overflowed its banks. One hundred twenty people baptized with the Holy Spirit. The sound of radical Christianity spilled out into the streets.

A crowd developed. First three hundred, then nine hundred. And then thousands. Enough to take an offering. Enough to "have church" if they only had a preacher. Well, they didn't have time to start a seminary. They needed action, now! Peter would do. He walked to the front.

Still, this was not church as usual. No slogans. No programs for the sake of programs. Peter, the one who had denied the Master, spoke with Holy Spirit power. He took his texts from the prophet Joel and the Psalms. He concluded with a clear invitation to change: "Repent and be baptized." And three thousand or so believed him.

It wasn't safe and secure for Christians anywhere. If you signed on for The Climb, it meant holding on to him for dear life. You never knew what to expect. You might get locked up for what you believed. But then again, the prison doors might mysteriously swing open and let you walk out, too. It was dangerous to go to sleep in church. You might fall out a window and kill yourself. But then again, the preacher might just lay hands on you and raise you from the dead. You might get comfortable in your home church—

First Church of Jerusalem—but watch out! Any time you think the world revolves around "our church," don't be surprised if God moves into Antioch and starts a church that would revolve around the world.

Tradition says that after the Antioch church formed, early Christians greeted one another with reciprocal declarations. When believers met together, one of them would say, "He is risen!" and the other would respond, "He is risen, indeed!" If you try that today—try walking down the streets of any American city—and approach the first person you meet and say, "He is risen," what do you suppose would be their reply? A look, probably. Either a suspicious look that says, "What are you? A nut?" or more likely, a look-the-other-way look—one of those "Maybe if I ignore him he'll go away" looks. For most of us, all it takes to cause us to keep our mouths shut in public about our Lord is a "look." Maybe we'd be more effective if we *looked* like those early believers.

I think they looked every day. I like to imagine that those early believers in Jerusalem took a walk every day for months and months after the resurrection. Not just an ambling walk. A purpose-filled walk, with a particular route in mind. They had to walk through the streets, of course. But then, they moved beyond their neighborhoods through the city gates.

I think they climbed the site where they crucified the Lord and stood there on that awful hill, looking. I think they looked past their own lives, past their own agendas, and beyond the things they once thought were important. They looked out at the lost world around them.

And then, I think they climbed down off that hill and decided to go do something about it.

But on their way to a lost world, they made one more stop. They walked by that empty tomb. And they stared at that place where the Word first got out—the living Word himself. Maybe they climbed up on that rock—the one he rolled away—and leaned back and stretched out to enjoy the Son. They may have even brought their lunch, just to savor the moment. I can picture those men and women in my mind as they sat there looking at that empty hole . . . smiling to themselves, thinking to themselves, talking to themselves . . . about something they just couldn't keep to themselves.

"He did it! My God, he actually did it! Risen from the dead . . . indeed."

Epilogue
The Climb of Your Life

Randee rummaged through a box of some old school papers of hers the other night; as a longtime teacher, she has all kinds of things she's saved from former students. In one particular envelope, she discovered some writing assignments she had given to some of her pupils several years ago. She taught high school students with special learning needs at the time. She gave the kids an assignment to write a one-page story about something that had actually happened to them. She collected the stories and then put them in the envelope and forgot she even had them.

I sat and watched her face as she read what some of her kids had written. Many of them used very simple language. Their punctuation needed work. Their sentences contained awkward constructions. These special education students did their best, though. And I could tell by her reactions to the simple, short stories that she felt great reward in just reading them.

But she discovered an interesting thing as she read through all the stories. When each student had finished writing his or her story, the teen wrote *The End* at the bottom of the page. There must have been thirty stories; thirty different kids who all did the assignment, and then wrote *The End* at the bottom of the page. All but one student. Our son, Nathan, was a part of the special education class my wife had taught. He did that same writing assignment, too. But when he finished his work, Nathan used a different finish than all the other kids.

It must not have occurred to Nathan to write *The End,* so instead he wrote another word—fewer letters, really. He wrote the word *Done*. When Randee showed me his paper, I sat for many moments and pondered such profound writing by our second son. I learn a lot by just being around my children, I guess.

Simeon, our youngest son, attends Seattle Pacific University, and we have learned much from him, too. But there are times when Simeon makes his mother and me very nervous.

She thinks he's not eating enough fresh vegetables. And that he doesn't wear his winter coat and hat enough. It gets cold in the winter in Seattle, you know. He called the other night to mention it. Said he nearly froze on his way to work. He was on the bus heading downtown when he reached his transfer point. Just as the bus pulled up to the transfer point and Simeon disembarked, the other bus he planned to board left the curb. The driver, oblivious to our son's shouts, pulled away and drove up the street.

Simeon sprinted four blocks up and down those hills in the freezing rain before he "caught that stupid bus!" (an exact quote). I guess I probably don't worry about the same sorts of things my wife does, but I am occasionally concerned. When he calls about his German class, I worry whether he's burning the midnight oil. (I wonder if any other SPU dads wish their kids were a little more "sleepless in Seattle"?)

Quite honestly, our concerns probably aren't any greater than any other parent whose kid leaves home for college. It's just that, even though Simeon is a great kid and very responsible, Mom and Dad still have those gnawing concerns.

That's why I picked it up. I picked something up as I walked across the campus when Randee and I dropped Simeon off last fall.

In those last few hours of our time together on the SPU campus, we did so many delightful things. We attended banquets and informative meetings designed to let us know what our kid would be doing throughout the school year. We went to see his apartment and helped him get things settled. We just wanted to familiarize ourselves with where our son would be living while we were apart. We walked all over campus, visiting the bookstore, the student union, the library.

During one of our strolls, before I got too side-tracked with other things, I stopped long enough to pick up a "memory stone." I noticed some buck-eyes covering the ground. Round, deep mahogany brown in color, about the size of a chestnut. Every fall, the SPU campus is covered with them. And I picked one up and showed it to Simeon.

"Sim," I said. "I'm putting this buckeye in my pocket as a prayer reminder for you. I promise never to let it leave my possession as long as you are away at school. And every time I put my hand in my pocket and touch this buckeye, I will think of you. And I will *never* think of you without praying for you."

And Simeon said thank you. And we walked on.

I write to Simeon nearly every day; e-mail is a wonderful thing. Right after my Bible reading and journaling time, I sit at my computer and write a brief note that I then e-mail to him. And never once have I forgotten to sign my letter with two inscriptions.

One of them is predictable, I suppose. But the other one may be peculiar to me and my three boys. I have been using the good-bye message with them for as long as I can remember. When they leave the house in a car. When they go on a date with girl. In the everyday-ness of coming and going to work, or school, or anywhere, as we part company I always say the same thing to them:

"I love you. *Don't forget who you belong to.*"

And they say, "Okay, Dad. I won't." And even when I write my son Simeon, I never forget. I close my letters with an abbreviation, a code between us.

Love,

Dad

DFWYBT

And Simeon knows exactly what I mean.

You've nearly read it all, all of one writer's thoughts on The Climb of your life. But this writer knows well that he has not said it all. I have hardly scratched the surface on all that could be said about the challenges and thrills and mysteries of life with him. Believe me, I would love to be able to give a deep and full answer to the mysteries of commitment. An answer so complete that gurus and governments would sit and marvel. But I'm afraid as soon as ABC News or CNN showed up and started investigating my credentials, credibility would be an immediate issue.

Confession time. I haven't got it all figured out. I still struggle with the really simple stuff. (I can't even keep my commitment to get the garbage can out in front of our house every Monday morning—or is it Tuesday?) I've tried to tell you some of my stories, but I still struggle with punctuating my life properly with prayer. I'm terribly prone to use passive constructions in my life, when God would love to see some action. I'm a pastor, not a lawmaker or a theorist. And I'm not a very good theologian, either, I suppose. I'm just a storyteller. And a dad, and a husband. A fellow struggler, trying to get a solid foothold on the incredibly exciting slopes of The Climb.

And I truly believe that as God sees us, his "living letters, known and read by all men," he takes great delight in our transparent disclosures and attempts at growth. I agree with Nathan's great observation on his writing assignment when he wrote the word *Done*. *The End* never comes when we belong to him. Have you heard? Of his kingdom, there shall be no end. Even if we die, we live. He may say the word some day, and I'll be "done" with one page of his plan for me, but I'm convinced there's no end to the glories that await us at the top of The Climb. He can hardly wait to see us.

In these parting moments, let me just encourage you, friend. While he was here among us, there was never a day that he wasn't thinking about you and me, and all the difficulties and challenges and temptations we face in The Climb. He didn't worry, of course. He controls it all. But that didn't keep him from committing to pray for us until we finish The Climb. He's at the Father's side, interceding for we who are his climbing companions. It's important to remember who you belong to—and that he cares for those who belong to him.

Yes, the Master will intercede. Want to know why I'm so sure he won't forget to pray? Well, while he was here visiting, and just before he left to go home, he stooped down; he picked something up that would remind him. The old prophet saw the whole thing.

"Can a mother forget the baby at her breast, and have no compassion on the child she has borne? Though she may forget, I will not forget you! See, I have engraved you on the palms of my hands" (Isa. 49:16).

I like to imagine that every time Jesus notices the scars in his hands, he thinks of me. And he never thinks of me without praying for me.

I close, then, with a reminder. Not my own words, but the words of an old warhorse:

> Brothers, we do not want you to be ignorant about those who fall asleep, or to grieve like the rest of men, who have no hope. We believe that Jesus died

and rose again, and so we believe that God will bring with Jesus those who have fallen asleep in him. According to the Lord's own word, we tell you that we who are still alive, who are left till the coming of the Lord, will certainly not precede those who have fallen asleep. For the Lord himself will come down from heaven with a loud command, with the voice of the archangel, and with the trumpet call of God, and the dead in Christ will rise first. After that, we who are still alive and are left will be caught up together with them in the clouds to meet the Lord in the air. And so we will be with the Lord forever. Therefore, encourage each other with these words.

1 Thessalonians 4:13–18

Almost home, friend. Keep climbin' and I'll see you at the top.

Love,
KJ
DFWYBT
Done . . . but not the end!

Notes

Chapter 4: Radical Lessons

1. The Beatitudes of Jesus are in Matthew 5:3–10; Jesus' words are from *The Message*, by Eugene Peterson (Colorado Springs: NavPress, 1993).

Chapter 11: White Space

1. Robert A. Rosenstone, *Mirror in the Stone*, as quoted in Doris Grumbach, *Fifty Days of Solitude* (Boston: Beacon, 1994), 24.
2. Thomas Szasz, *The Second Sin*, as quoted in Doris Grumbach, *Fifty Days of Solitude*, 16.

Chapter 16: Final Assault on the Summit

1. Calvin Miller, *The Singer* (Downers Grove, Ill.: InterVarsity, 1975), 69.

Chapter 17: Requiem

1. Walter Wangerin, Jr., *Miz Lil & the Chronicles of Grace* (San Francisco: Harper & Row, 1988), 184.

Ken Jones is available to speak at retreats and seminars on men's issues, parenting, marriage and family, or at writing conferences. His address is:

Ken Jones
c/o Watermark Ministries
P.O. Box 578413
Modesto, CA 95357

kdjones@s2.sonnet.com